G000113930

DAVID &
CHARLES
BRITAIN

THE
Pembrokeshire Coast National Park

THE
Pembrokeshire Coast
National Park

Dillwyn Miles

David & Charles
Newton Abbot   London   North Pomfret (Vt)

For Anthony

More titles in this series:
The Yorkshire Dales
Geoffrey N. Wright

Snowdonia
William Condry

Forthcoming titles:
The Lake District
Michael Dunn

The Northumbrian Uplands
Geoffrey N. Wright

British Library Cataloguing in Publication Data

Miles, Dillwyn
    The Pembrokeshire Coast National Park. ——
    (David & Charles' Britain)
    1. Pembrokeshire Coast National Park
    (Wales) —— Guide-books
    I. Title
    914.29′6204858   DA740.P3

ISBN 0-7153-8748-0

Phototypeset by ABM Typographics, Hull
Printed in Great Britain
by Butler & Tanner Ltd, Frome
for David & Charles Publishers plc
Brunel House   Newton Abbot   Devon

Published in the United States of America
by David & Charles Inc
North Pomfret   Vermont 05053   USA

CONTENTS

ACKNOWLEDGEMENTS

The author wishes to thank the following for permission to reproduce photographs: The Countryside Commission, J. W. Donovan, John L. Jones, B. R. Munt, Wales Tourist Board, and Roger Worsley.

He is indebted to Nic Wheeler, National Park Officer, and to John Evans, Roger Hiscock and Geraint Jones, of the staff of the Pembrokeshire Coast National Park Committee; to David Saunders, Administrative Officer, West Wales Trust for Nature Conservation; and to Peter Davies, OBE, Managing Director, Pembrokeshire Business Initiative, for their advice and assistance. He is particularly grateful to Amanda George and May Evans for their care in typing the manuscript, and to his editor and to Judith Graham-Jones for words of encouragement.

FOREWORD: MY NATIONAL PARK

In a remote valley in the heart of Snowdonia there lived an old shepherd who, according to one of our poets, though he owned not a foot-span of land, felt, as he sat by his fire of an evening, that he was lord of that valley. It is with that same humble sense of possession that I speak of the Pembrokeshire Coast National Park as mine.

I was born on the coast of north Pembrokeshire and, for as long as I can remember, I have walked along the edge of restless waters and over tall cliffs, leaning into the wind that made boiling cauldrons of the seas below; watched the sun slowly subside beyond a distant horizon into a backdrop of inferno, and gone to sleep to the garrulous vespers of sea-birds. I have meandered through oak-hung valleys while mewing buzzards wheeled in the summer haze, and lingered by tinkling streams where brown trout shimmered and dragonflies hovered beside the yellow iris. I have tramped through the purple and gold of heather and gorse across the Presely Hills, and felt the strange primeval sanctity that presides among them.

When I returned to Pembrokeshire after the war, one of my main ambitions in becoming a member of the County Council was to conserve the beauty and character of the area so that it would remain unspoilt for others to enjoy. Soon there were rumours that the Pembrokeshire coast might be designated a national park and when the Minister of Town and Country Planning, Dr Hugh Dalton, visited the county in May 1951, it was considered that he would make a declaration to that effect. It became apparent, however, that he was there to enjoy one of

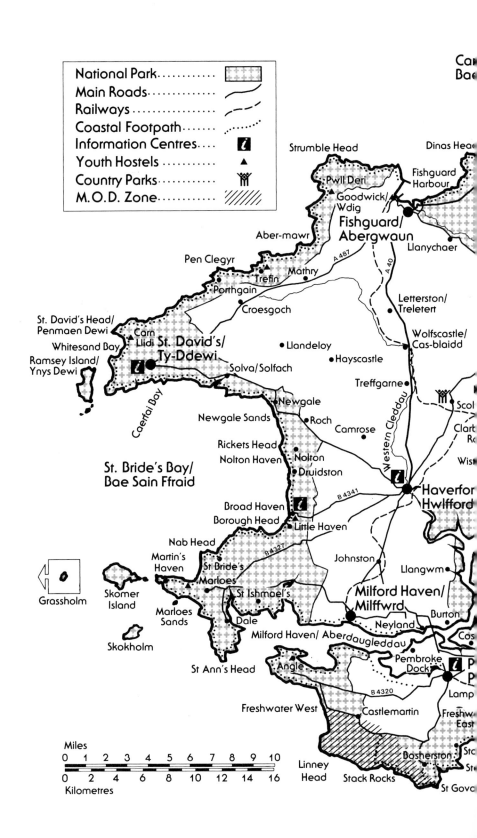

Pen Cemais

Cardigan/
Aberteifi

St. Dogmael's/
Llandudoch

ay/
igion

Moylegrove/
Trewyddel

Cilgerran

Afon
Teifi

Cenarth

Nevern/
Nyfer

Felindre Farchog

A 487

Newport/
Trefdraeth

Eglwyswrw

Boncath

Carn Ingli

alley/
aun

Preşely Hills/
Bryniau Presely

Freni Fawr

Crymych

Rosebush

Llanfyrnach

Maenclochog

A 478

Eastern
Cleddau

Country Park

y Park

Llandysilio

Llanboidy

Clunderwen

haden

eston Wathen

A 40

Whitland/
Hendy-gwyn

St. Clears/
Sancler

Narberth

Tavernspite

Templeton

letwy

Pendine

Begelly

Kilgetty/

Amroth

nny

West
illiamston

A 477

Wiseman's Bridge

Saundersfoot

Carew

New Hedges

Monkstone
Point

Carmarthen Bay/
Bae Caerfyrddin

e/

St. Florence

Tenby/
Dinbych-y-pysgod

Manorbier

Penally

Lydstep

Old Castle Head

Caldey Island

ead

his annual Whitsuntide expeditions to the remoter parts of Britain, along with his Parliamentary friends Arthur Blenkinsop, Geoffrey de Freitas and Barbara Castle. During our walk round the coast the Minister endlessly expressed his delight with all he saw, but made no declaration.

On 28 January 1952 Harold M. Abrahams, Secretary of the National Parks Commission, and Lord Merthyr, a member of the Commission and a former member of the Pembrokeshire County Council, came to meet the County Planning Committee and, having heard what they had to say, we decided 'to set up a new Committee to be called the Pembrokeshire National Park Committee'. The Park was officially designated on 29 February 1952. The new Committee was fortunate in having the County Planning Officer, the late John Price, as its first National Park Officer, and it was largely due to his acumen and diplomacy that the notion, and the disciplines, of a National Park received public acceptance.

Lord Merthyr also outlined to the County Planning Committee 'proposals for the establishment of a footpath round the Pembrokeshire coast as a long-distance route', and a preliminary survey was carried out by the naturalist R. M. Lockley. A decision to establish the path was taken in July 1953 but its completion was long delayed by the obstinacy of a small number of landowners. It was eventually declared open by Wynford Vaughan-Thomas, then President of the Council for the Protection of Rural Wales, at a ceremony held above Monkstone Point on 16 May 1970.

This book is about the Pembrokeshire Coast National Park, which includes most of the coast, the Presely Hills and reaches of the Daugleddau, but I confess to having strayed occasionally across its boundaries, for a sight is no less beautiful, or a place less absorbing, because it is the other side of an imaginary line.

Haverfordwest   Dillwyn Miles

INTRODUCTION

Where the old road from Haverfordwest to Cardigan crosses the Presely Hills at Bwlch-gwynt, 'the windy pass', a path leads westward across the heather towards the summit of Foel Eryr. From here, on a clear day, your eye will follow the horizon and see, towards the east, a patchwork of countryside leading to the Black Mountains; towards the south, Dunkery Beacon rising beyond the Bristol Channel; westward, the gold-bearing hills of Wicklow, and to the north, Bardsey, the Lleyn Peninsula and the peaks of Snowdonia.

Look closer, and you will see Pembrokeshire around you: the cockscomb of Carn Ingli, fortress of the war-like Celts; the great maw of St Bride's Bay, shimmering silver between the St David's Peninsula, the seat of Welsh Christianity, and the tall stacks that symbolise modern industry in the region of Milford Haven; the hills of Presely named, they say, after one Solomon, his wood, but Solomon the King in all his glory was no match for the hills when they are clothed in the purple and gold of heather and gorse; the green pastures of the south that were quickly seized by the Normans, and just as quickly defended by so many castles that Pembrokeshire was known as the county of castles.

Pembrokeshire has always been one of the remote places of Britain. Ever a sea-girt promontory, separated from the rest of Wales by a veil of mystery, it was known from earliest time as *gwlad hud a lledrith,* the land of magic and enchantment. True, it was known to prehistoric man, who considered the bluestones of Presely sufficiently sacred to be trans-

Ordovician folds at Ceibwr, with Pen-yr-afr beyond (*B. R. Munt*)

ported to Salisbury Plain, eventually to become part of the wonder of Stonehenge. Early Christian saints also knew it, as it lay on the route of their unending travels between Ireland and Rome. To most outsiders throughout the centuries, however, it was tantamount to *ultima Thule.*

Those who came and saw they could go no further called it *Pen bro,* which was softly mutated, as is the way in the Welsh language, to *Penfro,* and anglicised as *Pembroke.*

Its people have always been close to the land, rearing cattle and sheep, and turning the soil so as to grow corn and, more latterly, potatoes. They have been close also to the sea, harvesting its fish and, as sailors, bringing home the spices of India and the silks of Cathay. Industry began at home with spinning and weaving, and spread only to the corn mill, the cloth factory and the stone quarry. For a time, there was also a flourishing coal industry producing some of the finest anthracite in the world. Later, in the sixties, new demands for energy brought oil refineries and a power station to Milford Haven.

The scenic beauty and the bracing air of Pembrokeshire made it increasingly popular as a holiday resort during the last two centuries and led to the growth of a prosperous tourist industry. Tenby began to find favour as a resort for seaside holidays in the middle of the eighteenth century. A small chapel on the harbour wall, used by fishermen for prayers, was converted in 1781 by an apothecary from Haverfordwest into a bathing-house for the use of patients to whom he had prescribed the benefit of sea water. So successful was the venture that he soon extended his scheme and, encouraged by his example, speculators began to erect houses above the cliffs to accommodate summer visitors. In 1805 Sir William Paxton built a more fashionable bathing-house, designed by the architect S. P. Cockerell and fitted with dressing-rooms, a lounge and 'a spacious vestibule for servants to wait in, without mixing with the company'. Over the door were carved, in the original Greek, appropriate words from Euripides's *Iphigenia in Aulis*, 'the sea washeth away the ills of men'.

The desire to make the countryside available for the enjoyment of its natural beauty, and as a place of relaxation for town-dwellers, gained currency during the early part of the last century. William Wordsworth envisaged the Lake District as 'a sort of national property in which every man has an interest who has an eye to perceive and a heart to enjoy'. At the same time, people in towns formed groups to pursue country interests and the study of wild life.

Meanwhile, in the United States the idea of a national park was evolved with the establishment of the Yellowstone National Park in 1872. It was not until 1949, however, that an Act of Parliament reached the statute book providing for the designation of national parks in England and Wales. The Peak District was so designated in 1951, followed by the Lake District, Snowdonia and Dartmoor and, in February 1952, by the Pembrokeshire Coast National Park.

'No part of the coastline of England and Wales is more beautiful or more interesting than that of Pembrokeshire', wrote the great authority on the coasts of Britain, Professor J. A. Steers. The Pembrokeshire Coast National Park is more than coastline, however, for it also includes the well wooded reaches of the Daugleddau and the bare uplands of the Presely Hills. The hills form the backbone of Pembrokeshire and stretch from Freni Fach and Freni Fawr, which are to the east of the National Park, to Foel Eryr and beyond, their rounded summits sometimes broken by rocky outcrops. The highest point, at Foel Cwm

Carreg Goetan Arthur, Newport. 'Arthur's Quoit' was a not uncommon name for a burial chamber (see page 32) (B. R. Munt)

Cerwyn, reaches only 1,760ft (537m), but the general impression is of a higher range of hills. Foel Drygarn has a crown of three Bronze Age cairns, hence its name, and an Iron Age fort surrounds its summit. From the ice-shattered rocks of Carn Alw and Carnmenyn came the bluestones of Stonehenge. The prehistoric ridgeway that runs the length of the hills may be trodden in one afternoon.

The whole of the coast of Pembrokeshire lies within the Park, with the exception of the area around Fishguard and Goodwick and the industrialised part of Milford Haven. Along the north coast, from Pen Cemais to Morfa Head, there are high cliffs of great splendour, often folded in strange and colourful shapes, standing over rocky shores where seals breed in autumn. Dinas Island, though no longer insulated, separates the wide bays of Newport and Fishguard, and bears the devil's footprints at its tip, they say. Strumble Head, strewn with prehistory, was also the scene of the last attempted invasion of Britain.

When Kilvert visited St David's in 1871 he wrote in his diary: 'And so we came to the end of the world where the Patron Saint of Wales sleeps by the western sea.' The peninsula, the most westerly in Wales, was landfall for early Christian missionaries who built chapels in thankfulness for having escaped 'the eight perils', the perilous offshore islands. Ynys Dewi, David's island, re-named Ramsey by the Norse, in honour of one Hrafn, is protected by sheer cliffs and treacherous seas. No sea knows greater fury than that which surges through Ramsey Sound in a winter's gale.

The Park boundary travels eastward and nearer to the coast as it passes the sheltered inlet of Solva, and excludes Brawdy Airfield before it turns south to follow the softer shores of St Bride's Bay. The great stretch of Newgale Sands is backed on its northern half by a mile-long storm beach. The Welsh Way, the road that hugs the coast, then follows rising ground and provides spectacular views across St Bride's Bay before returning to sea level at Nolton Haven. There are traces of coal-working, for the Pembrokeshire coalfield here reached the coast, and there are millions of tons of coal still unworked under the sea. Broad Haven has long been a favourite family resort, and Little Haven is popular both for bathing and sailing.

The whole of the Marloes peninsula lies within the Park. The road through the village of Marloes leads to Martin's Haven, departure point for the islands of Skomer and Skokholm, and to the Deer Park. This overlooks the turbulent and treacherous waters of Jack Sound, that separate it from Skomer, and provides a panoramic view of the wide expanse of St Bride's Bay and Skokholm southwards across Broad Sound. Beyond Great Marloes Sands, with its backdrop of up-ended Silurian strata, is the Dale Peninsula which was an off-shore island in preglacial times when the sea ran through the valley between Westdale Bay and Dale village. St Ann's Head, with its cliff-top lighthouse, stands where beacons have stood for centuries guiding the mariner through dangerous reefs into the safety of Milford Haven.

The Park enters the Haven to include Sandy Haven and South Hook Point on the north side, and goes as far as Pwllcrochan, beyond Angle and the Texaco Oil Refinery, on the south shore. The high ground of the Angle Peninsula provides good views of the Haven, and of Thorn Island upon which stands a Victorian fort converted into an hotel, accessible by boat from West Angle Bay.

Beyond the great sweep of Freshwater West, one of the finest beaches on the Welsh coast, the National Park is closed to the public as it forms part of the Castlemartin Royal Armoured Corps firing ranges, and the splendour of the coastline, with its magnificent limestone cliffs reach-

Porth Clais, medieval port of the monastic community at St David's (*B. R. Munt*)

ing westward to Linney Head, may only be appreciated from the Stack Rocks, where the prohibition ends during non-firing periods. The tall cliffs continue eastward, however, from St Govan's Head, the most southerly point of Pembrokeshire. From these there are extensive views over the Bristol Channel including the Gower Peninsula, the island of Lundy and the coast of Somerset and Devon.

The three-fingered lily pools at Bosherston are cut off from the sea by a bank of shingle and sand dunes that back the golden beach of Broad Haven South. The beach at Barafundle Bay is accessible only by foot and remains unspoilt. The Park boundary narrowly misses the Bishop's Palace at Lamphey, where the Earl of Essex, Elizabeth's favourite, spent his youth, but well and truly includes Manorbier, that stands above the sea like a Crusader castle of the Levant. It was from here that Giraldus Cambrensis, a son of the castle, set out to preach the Third Crusade.

Tenby is the largest town within the National Park, with a population of 5,000, that doubles, or even trebles, during the high season. It provides for all the needs of holiday makers and yet retains a medieval air within its embattled walls. Saundersfoot, by contrast, is comparatively new: it came into being as a harbour for the export of coal and iron but is now a highly popular resort and a haven for pleasure craft.

The sands continue, with rocky interruptions, and may be followed at low tide, all the way to Amroth, where the National Park ends at a stream which marked the boundary of the former county of Pembroke. The coast path which begins here follows the coast for 180 miles (290km), except where the Castlemartin ranges intervene, to St Dogmael's.

The Daugleddau sector of the National Park begins beyond the Cleddau Bridge and extends along the Western Cleddau almost as far as Haverfordwest and along the Eastern Cleddau to Canaston Bridge, and includes the estuaries of the Carew and Cresswell rivers. Within its boundary lie Carew Castle, once the scene of a great tournament, Upton Castle, with its splendid woodland of diverse trees and shrubs, and Picton Castle, attached to which is the Graham Sutherland Gallery. The beauty of the area can best be enjoyed by taking a boat trip along the river, travelling between fields that reach down to the water's edge and hanging oakwoods, from which peers the white tower of Benton Castle. Lawrenny is a leading yachting centre.

When the Pembrokeshire Coast National Park was so designated it was assumed that it would be inviolable for all time. It soon became apparent, however, that the government intended to take advantage of the deep and sheltered waterway of Milford Haven to bring in the giant tankers that were being built to carry large tonnages of oil round the Cape of Good Hope. The National Park Authority was faced with the task of accommodating the Esso Refinery on the shores of the Haven and, almost simultaneously, the building of an oil terminal that was to be connected by underground pipeline to the BP Refinery, 60 miles (95km) away at Llandarcy. There followed the Texaco, the Gulf Oil and the Amoco refineries. In 1975 the oil-fired Pembroke Power station, one of the largest in Europe, was built, and massive metal pylons strode the countryside carrying supergrid power lines towards England. While these developments brought employment, much of it imported and temporary, they presented serious problems to the Authority in its youthful days. However, with careful planning and the willing co-operation of the oil companies, the refineries were discreetly arranged so as to cause the least damage to the landscape.

Although the extent of afforestation within the Park is small, covering only 3 per cent of its total area, the plantation of stands of conifers on the Presely Hills has been a cause of concern. The Authority has consistently discouraged coniferous plantations and fostered the reten-

North Beach, Tenby, with Gosker Rock (*Countryside Commission*)

tion, and extension, of deciduous woodland, and has provided an advisory service on forestry management.

The Authority was unable to assess, at the outset, the future demand for holiday accommodation. A rough survey carried out in 1952 indicated that accommodation for 10,000 persons was to be had in hotels, guesthouses and private houses within the county of Pembroke, and that half of it was in the Tenby area. There was hardly a reference to caravan sites in that survey. Today the accommodation available at hotels, guesthouses, farmhouses and other establishments is considerably increased, and there are nearly 10,000 permitted pitches for caravans. It is estimated that 1½ million people visit the National Park each year for their holidays, a fifth of whom come from other parts of Wales, and a further fifth each from south-east England and the West Midlands. The main reasons given by visitors for the visit are enjoyment of the beaches, general sightseeing and the coastal scenery.

The praises of Pembrokeshire have long been sung. In the twelfth century Giraldus Cambrensis described it as 'the finest part of the province of Dyfed' which itself was 'the most beautiful' part of Wales. Four centuries later George Owen of Henllys wrote 'in praise and worthiness of the people and the county', and marvelled at 'the divers wonders of Pembrokeshire'.

1
THE SHAPE OF PEMBROKESHIRE

Pembrokeshire, it has been said, is a geologist's paradise. Nowhere in so compact an area is there a greater diversity of rock formation, ranging from crystalline volcanics disgorged when the earth was young to seams of coal laid down in recent geological time. Nowhere, in consequence, is there a richer variety of scenic and natural beauty. (There is a glossary of geological terms at the end of this chapter).

Its geological features were noted by Giraldus Cambrensis in the twelfth century and, four centuries later, in considerably more detail by George Owen of Henllys, who traced rock formations and 'discerned the meaning of a geological map'. Those who studied the older rocks during the eighteenth and nineteenth centuries did so in Wales and gave them names that had Welsh associations: Pre-Cambrian, Cambrian, Ordovician, Silurian. Furthermore, the extrusive igneous Pre-Cambrian rocks, formed by the solidification of lava above the earth's surface, were called Pebidian, after the Welsh hundred of Pebidiog that lay around St David's, while the intrusive igneous rocks of that period, composed of magma that solidified subterraneously, became known as Dimetian, from Demetia, the Latin form of Dyfed. Cambrian rocks were categorised as the Caerfai, Solva and Menevian series, and a series of the Ordovician system was named Llanvirn after a farm near Abereiddi.

The Pebidian are exposed along the anticline of the St David's Peninsula, in the cliffs facing Ramsey Sound, and above Ogof Morgan (SM 720233), and again in the parallel anticlines running through

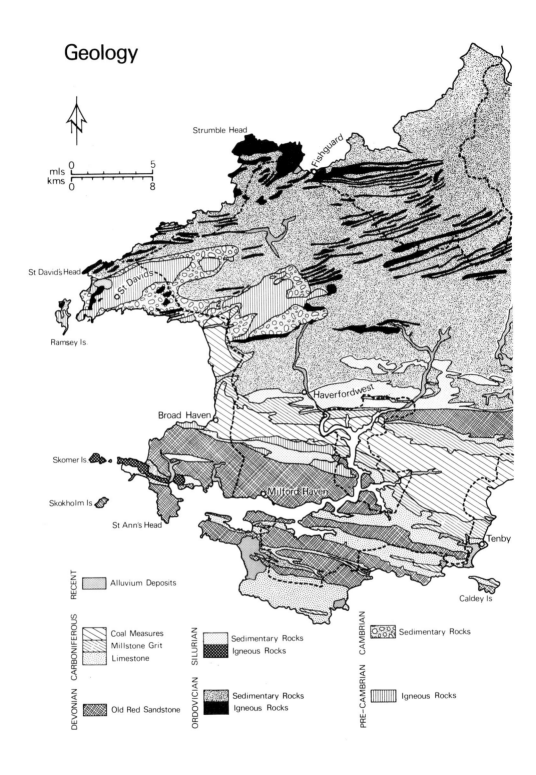

Geology

Strumble Head

Fishguard

St David's Head

St Davids

Ramsey Is.

Broad Haven

Haverfordwest

Skomer Is.

Skokholm Is

Milford Haven

St Ann's Head

Tenby

Caldey Is

RECENT	Alluvium Deposits

CARBONIFEROUS	Coal Measures
	Millstone Grit
	Limestone
DEVONIAN	Old Red Sandstone

SILURIAN	Sedimentary Rocks
	Igneous Rocks
ORDOVICIAN	Sedimentary Rocks
	Igneous Rocks

CAMBRIAN	Sedimentary Rocks
PRE-CAMBRIAN	Igneous Rocks

mls 0   5
kms 0   8

Hayscastle and Treffgarne, and about Benton Castle. Roch Castle stands upon a crag of resistant rhyolite, which also appears in magnificent shapes at Maiden Castle and Poll Carn above Treffgarne Gorge. Dimetian granites form small outcrops to the south-west and north-east of St David's, and near Brawdy and Hayscastle. Pre-Cambrian outcrops to the east and west of Johnston are probably older even than those of the St David's Peninsula.

The Cambrian rocks are formed of sediments that accumulated on the Pre-Cambrian when the region was drowned by an advancing sea. They are well displayed on the south shore of Whitesand Bay and along the north coast of St Bride's Bay. The red shales of the Caerfai series, conspicuous in Caerfai Bay and at Cwm Mawr, near Newgale, are the oldest fossilbearing rocks, and the plum-coloured sandstone at Caerbwdi was quarried and used in the construction of St David's Cathedral. The dark mudstones of Porth-y-rhaw (SM 786242) yielded the enormous trilobite *Paradoxides davidis* measuring 2ft (60cm).

The steep dip of the older, Lower Cambrian rocks, exposed between Porth Clais and Porth-y-rhaw, is the southern slope of the massive anticline of the St David's Peninsula: the northern slope is visible at the north end of Whitesand Bay. George Owen in the sixteenth century noted that the stony soil produced by the Cambrian sedimentary rocks made Dewsland 'very fruitful of corn, especially barley'.

The greater part of north Pembrokeshire, however, is of Ordovician rocks, including sandstones and grits and great thicknesses of shale, deposited around 500 million years ago, along with accumulations of lava and volcanic ash produced by igneous activity in the Ordovician sea, with volcanic cones emerging as islands. Lava extruded in this sea cooled rapidly into globular masses which appear as the basaltic pillows (pillow lava) near Strumble Head lighthouse that are known locally as *torthau ceiniogau*, 'penny loaves'. At Pen Anglas (SM 948405) the cooling of the molten rock caused columnar jointing in the dolerite rocks, producing a scene that is reminiscent of the Giant's Causeway. The intrusive igneous rocks are exposed in narrow strips and, owing to their resistant nature, commonly form headlands along the north-west coast, where bays and inlets cut into the softer Ordovician shales. Abereiddi bay is eroded into Llanvirn and Llandeilo shales that contain the tuning-fork graptolites *Didymograptus bifidii* and *Didymograptus Murchisoni*. The monadnocks of Carn Llidi, Pen Beri and Garn-fawr have resisted erosion and, at one time, stood out as islands in the Ordivician sea. (The term 'monadnock' comes from Mount Monadnock in New Hampshire, a plug of Ordovician igneous rock.)

Resistant rhyolitic rock at Treffgarne (*John L. Jones*)

Sills of dolerite appear abundantly in the Presely Hills and contribute to their mountain form. The outcrops in the Carn Menyn area (SN 144324), with their characteristic pink and white spots, were identified as the source of the bluestones of Stonehenge.

In south Pembrokeshire there are narrow Ordovician exposures at Marloes and in the Castlemartin Peninsula, and also in the core of the Freshwater East anticline. The igneous rocks stretching westward from Wooltack to Skomer, Grassholm and The Smalls were previously regarded as Ordovician but they are now considered to be early Silurian and provide the only signs of volcanic activity during this period.

A coastal belt extending from the Teifi estuary to Newport Bay, and the tip of Dinas Head, shown on most geological maps as Ordovician, has proved to be a Silurian outcrop, separated by the Ordovician from the Silurian exposures of mid-Pembrokeshire, where the Haverfordwest Gasworks mudstones yield brachiopods, trilobites, corals and the screw-like *Tentaculites*. Silurian sedimentary rocks at Marloes and Wooltack rest on the Skomer volcanic rocks, and appear exposed in the cliffs between The Anvil (SM 756088) and Marloes Sands where some of the strata, notably the Three Chimneys, stand on end. A thin strip stretches from Freshwater West to Freshwater East.

Towards the end of the Silurian period, about 400 million years ago, the geography of Pembrokeshire was transformed by the intense earth movements of the Caledonian orogeny, which caused great folding and large-scale faulting of the rocks. Surfaces that had lain under the sea for millions of years were uplifted and folded, and the topography of north Pembrokeshire acquired its west-south-west and east-north-east trend.

The material eroded from these uplifted surfaces by subaerial erosion was carried southward by torrential streams and spread as alluvial deposits to form the old red sandstone that covers wide areas of south Pembrokeshire. Red marls of the Lower old red sandstone are exposed on either side of Nab Head, around the Dale Peninsula, between Stackpole Quay and Old Castle Head, and on the rocky foreshore at Freshwater West, as well as at Gateholm and on Skokholm. At Skrinkle Haven the uppermost beds are interrupted by grey calcareous layers and include conglomerates that contain fragments of pre-Cambrian and Ordovician rocks. From the Cosheston beds in Milford Haven came the recumbent 16ft (5m) pillar of micaceous sandstone at Stonehenge which Inigo Jones named the 'Altar Stone'.

The alluvial beds of the Old Red Sandstone period were drowned close on 350 million years ago and, in a warm, shallow sea, the skeletal

Lydstep Point, with vertical bedding as a result of the Armorican earth movement (see opposite) (*Countryside Commission*)

debris of marine organisms led to the formation of carboniferous lime-stone which lies in belts across south Pembrokeshire and has its largest exposure along the south coast of the Castlemartin Peninsula, from Stackpole Head to Linney Head, providing one of the most magnificent stretches of limestone cliffs in Britain. The Green Bridge of Wales (SM 925944) will, one day, lose its elegant arch through erosion and become a pillar of rock, like the nearby Eligug Stack.

The millstone grit forms a long outcrop extending from Tenby to Johnston and is exposed on the foreshore of Tenby North Sands. A more extended outcrop runs from Marros Sands, east of Amroth, to Druidston Haven, and between these two outcrops lie the coal measures of the Pembrokeshire Coalfield, that are well exposed from Amroth to Monkstone Point (SN 151032) and along the coast of St Bride's Bay from Talbenny to Newgale.

Following the end of the Carboniferous period, about 300 million years ago, another earth movement occurred, albeit of a lesser intensity than the Caledonian. As it was centred locally in Brittany, it is known as the Armorican orogeny and its stresses produced the ridge-and-valley topography of south Pembrokeshire with its west-north-west and east-south-east trend.

There are only few traces of the period following this upheaval. Pockets of red marl, sandstones and breccias in the limestone, and notable in the cliffs between Lydstep and Skrinkle Haven and in Bullslaughter Bay, are probably of Triassic age. A unique area of white and mottled pipeclay resting on the limestone near Flimston is likely to have been deposited during the early Tertiary period. It has the remains of pits

Limestone cliff terrace at The Wash. Saddle Point, the most southerly point of Pembrokeshire can be seen in the distance (*Countryside Commission*)

Eligug Stack, its crown covered with 'eligugs' (guillemots) (*Countryside Commission*)

The Lady Cave anticline at Saundersfoot (*Countryside Commission*)

from which the clay was dug for the making of pottery and abrasive powder.

The landscape of Pembrokeshire today barely reflects its complicated geological history, as it has been eroded to produce near-flat land surfaces which appear at three levels, at intervals of approximately 200ft (60m) above sea level. This indicates that the land was uplifted from beneath the sea in a series of pulses to expose former sea floors, probably during the late Tertiary period. The steep slopes that separate these platforms are the remains of ancient cliff lines.

The 200ft (60m) platform is the most extensive and is a major feature of the National Park. It is best displayed in the south where it extends from Linney Head to Lydstep and across to Caldey, while further north the Dale Peninsula, the St David's Peninsula, Ramsey and Pen-caer have been planed to a similar level. The resistant igneous monadnocks of Carn Ysgubor, Carn Llundain, Carn Llidi, Penberi and Garn Fawr are the relics of higher platforms, and were once islands. Evidence of the 400ft (120m) platform is visible between Croesgoch and Mathry, and on Dinas Island, while traces of the 600ft (180m) platform appear to the north-east of Newport and along the southern margin of the Presely Hills, notably around Maenclochog, Llangolman and Efailwen.

On at least two occasions the land surface was subjected to glaciation. The first occurred about 120,000 years ago when the whole area lay under the Irish Sea Glacier that was of a thickness of more than 1,000 feet over the summits of Presely. The second glacial period reached its peak some 20,000 years ago and covered the northern part of Pembrokeshire. The landscape bears only slight evidence of the effect of these glacial invasions, however. Some hollows on the northern side of the Presely Hills were deepened by the erosive action of ice and snow and there are traces of small corrie glaciers. Frost-shattered rocks on Carn Menyn and Carn Alw provided ready made bluestone pillars for use in the building of Stonehenge. Evidence of ice movement appears in the striation (scratching) of rock surfaces at Whitesand Bay, on Carn Llidi near its summit, and in the widespread scatter of erratic stones (rocks broken away by a glacier and carried away to be deposited elsewhere when the ice melts). A large boulder that overhangs the extremity of St Govan's Head had its origin in Snowdonia, and one lying in the village of Bosherston was carried by ice from Scotland. Foreign stones brought by ice from the far north were used as tombstones in the graveyard of Flimston Chapel.

Sea-floor material was dredged by the glaciers and deposited as a dark purple till, or boulder clay, containing striated stones and fragments of

Geological Time Scale in Pembrokeshire

Era	Age in millions of years	Period or System
Cainozoic		Quarternary
	— 2 —	
		Tertiary
	— 65 —	
Mezozoic		Cretaceous Jurassic Triassic
	— 225 —	
Upper Palaeozoic		Permian
	— 280 —	
		Carboniferous
	— 345 —	
Lower Palaeozoic		Old Red Sandstone (Devonian)
	— 395 —	Silurian
	— 440 —	
		Ordovician
	— 500 —	
		Cambrian
Eozoic	— 570 —	
		Pre-Cambrian
	— 4,500 —	

There are no solid rocks in Pembrokeshire younger than the coal measures of the Carboniferous period, apart from a small patch of Tertiary pipeclay, of about 25 million years, near Flimston. Most of the unconsolidated sands, gravels, clays and other materials which cover the solid rock are less than 100 million years old. The oldest, the Pre-Cambrian rocks, are probably no older than 2,000 million years.

sea shells. Exposures of Irish Sea till appear at Aber Mawr, Porth Melgan, Whitesand Bay and Druidston Haven, and on moorland near St David's and Fishguard.

As the ice retreated, deep channels were cut by meltwater released by the glaciers, a most spectacular example of which is the complex channel system to the south and east of Fishguard, including the Gwaun Valley where a deep and steep-sided valley was cut across the uplands, separating Carn Ingli from the mass of the Presely Hills. Meltwater channels isolated Dinas Island and Barry Island, and their effect is to be seen at Merry Vale, St David's, and in the valley of the Solfach. The meltwater streams deposited vast quantities of sands and gravels on valley floors, which sometimes formed eskers (long ridges), as at Monington, or terraces, as at Mullock Bridge.

During the glacial periods, the sea level was lowered and river valleys then formed were later drowned to form rias (drowned valleys) as the sea level rose again with the melting of the ice. Milford Haven and its tidal tributaries had their lower reaches drowned in this manner and similar, though smaller, drowned valleys appear at Newport, Aber Rhigian, Solva and Porth Clais, in the Ritec as far as St Florence, and at Bosherston Pools.

Raised beaches, with sand and pebbles resting on wave-cut platforms at Poppit, Ogof Golchfa (SM 742237) and at Broad Haven, near Bosherston, were formed during an interglacial period when the sea level was about twenty feet higher than at present.

When the ice of the last glaciation finally melted, around 6,000 years ago, the sea rose to its present level and, when tides are low, especially after winter storms, the remains of ancient forests are exposed on beaches at Newport, Aber Mawr, Whitesand, Newgale, Freshwater West, Freshwater East, Manorbier, Lydstep, Saundersfoot and Amroth. Flint artefacts found among the tree stumps indicate that early man stalked his quarry in these forests.

Glossary

Alluvial deposits   Sand and silt which a river has carried in suspension and which it has been forced to deposit.
Anticline   A fold or fold system, taking the form of an arch.
Boulder clay   Boulders and rocks embedded in silt clay. They were dragged along by glaciers and left behind by the melting retreating ice.

Brachiopods   A group of bivalved marine animals with shells, generally of unequal size, which have lived in all the geological periods from the Cambrian onwards.

Breccia   Rock consisting of angular fragments cemented together.

Columnar jointing   Polygonal jointing or fracture in igneous rocks resulting in a columnar structure.

Conglomerate   A hardened rock made up of pebbles cemented together.

Corals   Small marine animals with hard skeletons made of calcium carbonate.

Corrie   A deep, rounded hollow with steep sides, formed through erosion by snow and ice.

Dolerite   A basic coarse-grained igneous rock commonly occurring in dykes or sills.

Erosion   The general wearing away of rocks by weathering and the friction of material transported by water, ice or wind.

Fault   A fracture in the earth's crust along which movement has taken place.

Fold   A bend in stratified rocks caused by movements of the earth's crust.

Fossil   The remains of a once living animal or plant which has been buried and preserved for a long period in the rocks of the earth's crust.

Granite   A hard, coarse igneous rock containing quartz and feldspar and other minerals.

Graptolites   A group of extinct marine animals of uncertain affinity. The skeletons comprise one or more thread-like branches with rows or small cups along one or both sides giving minute saw-like edges.

Grit   Sandstone in which the grains are angular rather than rounded.

Igneous rocks   Rocks formed by the cooling and consequent solidification of molten magma (lava).

Jointing   Fracture in a rock between the sides of which, unlike a fault, little or no movement has taken place.

Lava   Molten rock (or magma) discharged from a volcano.

Limestone   Sedimentary rock rich in calcium carbonate, usually formed in warm, shallow water and very fossiliferous.

Magma   Molten material within the earth's crust which may consolidate to form igneous rock.

Mudstone   Sedimentary rock of hardened mud.

Orogeny   A period of mountain building during which areas of the earth's crust are thrown up into folds.

Rhyolite   Light-coloured volcanic rock, rich in quartz and feldspar, which occurs commonly in Ordovician igneous areas.

Sedimentary rocks   Rocks formed from material deposited as beds, or sediments under water, eg sandstone, mudstone, shale, together with material of organic origin, eg coal.

Shale   A fine-grained sedimentary rock produced from clay which readily splits into thin layers parallel to the bedding.

Trilobites   A group of extinct marine animals with external shell or carapace, abundant during the Cambrian period but declining gradually thereafter.

Volcanic ash   The unconsolidated finer-grained material thrown out by volcanic explosion.

Volcanic rocks   Rocks laid down as a result of volcanic action.

2
MAN IN PEMBROKESHIRE

Somewhere around 10,000 years ago, following upon the last Ice Age but while it was still cold, the first men came to Pembrokeshire and found shelter in Nanna's Cave on Caldey, Hoyle's Mouth and Longbury Bank near Tenby, and Catshole Quarry Cave on the Pembroke river. The food bones they left in the cave entrances indicate that they lived by hunting hoofed animals that grazed the tundra vegetation which covered the land, and which included areas that were later submerged as the ice melted and the sea level rose. Their implements, which may be seen at the Tenby Museum, suggest that they were connected with people who had developed a distinctive Old Stone Age culture, first identified in caves at Creswell Crags in Derbyshire.

As the climate grew warmer and wetter during the succeeding Mesolithic Age, men were able to settle on open sites along the coast. Traces of their occupation may be seen along the coastal footpath in the form of chipping floors, where small flints were fashioned so that they could be mounted on bone or antler to make weapons or implements for hunting and fishing. The main sites are at Nab Head (SM 791111), Little Furzenip (SR 886994), Swanlake (SS 042981) and Small Ord Point (SS 150966) on Caldey, but flint flakes are frequently found along other stretches of the west and south coasts. The only known site in the north is at Newport, on the estuary of the river Nevern (SN 062393). Many of their settlements were swamped as the

sea level continued to rise with the melting of the glaciers, and land surfaces over which they hunted their prey were submerged. Among the
bones of a wild pig found in the 'sunken forest' at Lydstep Haven were
flint arrowheads that appear to have found their target.

A completely new way of life was introduced by the Neolithic
people, who arrived about 5,000 years ago, bringing with them the arts
of agriculture. The only trace of their habitation found in Pembrokeshire is at Clegyr Boia (SM 737251) where the remains of a round hut
and a rectangular dwelling were discovered, along with stone axes and
pottery. Their reverence for the dead, however, is to be seen in the
great chambered tombs, or *cromlechau,* which they built as monuments. The *cromlech* consisted of a large capstone resting on three or
more supporters, the intervening spaces being filled with dry-stone walling to form the burial chamber. The whole was originally covered by a
mound of earth, or stones, but the covering has invariably been removed by the elements, or the hand of man, so that only the megaliths
remain, and these are sometimes damaged or collapsed. The tombs are
most numerous in the north, many of them near the coast, including
Llechydrybedd (SN 101432), Trellyffant (SN 082425), Carreg Goetan
Arthur, Newport (SN 059393), Cerrig y Gôf (SN 037389), Garn Wen
(SM 947390), Garn Wnda (SM 933393), Garn Gilfach (SM 908390),
Ffyst Samson (SM 906349), Carreg Samson (SM 848335), Carn Llidi
(SM 736279), and Carreg Goetan Arthur, St David's (SM 725281). In
the south are the King's Quoit (SS 059973) at Manorbier, and the
Devil's Quoit (SM 887008) on Broomhill Burrows.

Pentre Ifan (SN 099370) is one of the most spectacular burial chambers in the country. Its massive capstone is supported by three tall
uprights, with a fourth forming a portal at the south end, where several
additional stones, some now fallen, define a crescentic forecourt in
front of the chamber. These features, together with a few potsherds,
found when the tomb was excavated by Professor W. F. Grimes, link
the monument with the Irish court cairns and indicate a colonisation
from Ireland around 3000BC. Garne Turne (SM 981273), a collapsed
chamber, bears similar features, and Trellyffant, Cerrig y Gôf,
Ffynnondridian (SM 921365) and Tresewig (SM 827284) appear to be
related.

Another type of tomb had a polygonal chamber with access provided

Newgale Sands. The stack in the foreground is a silent reminder that coal was
mined here up to the present century (*Roger Worsley*)

by a passage-way, beneath a round mound, of which Carreg Samson, Llechydrybedd, Carreg Goetan Arthur at Newport, and the Hanging Stone (SM 972082) near Burton, are examples.

A third group has simple chambers with capstones supported on low uprights, or even on natural ledges of rock, but most of these are ruined and difficult to recognise. They include Garn Wen, Carn Wnda, Carn Gilfach, Carn Llidi, Carreg Goetan at St David's, and the King's Quoit at Manorbier.

The stone axes associated with the Neolithic dwellings at Clegyr Boia were of rhyolitic tuff and probably came from an axe-factory somewhere at the eastern end of the Presely Hills. Another factory, producing axes of spotted dolerite, was probably located in the bluestone area of Carn Menyn (SN 144326). The products of these factories are widely distributed and have been found as far afield as county Antrim in Ireland and, in particular, on Salisbury Plain.

Carn Menyn and the surrounding outcrops are the source of the foreign stones, or bluestones, at Stonehenge, erected about 2250BC. Over eighty of these stones, conveniently split by ice action, were brought on sledges to the tidal waters of the Eastern Cleddau and thence along the coast by water and up the Bristol Avon and the Frome, from where they were hauled overland to Warminster and floated down the Wylye. A bluestone boulder found in a long barrow at Heytesbury, on the Wylye, shows that such stones were being transported to this area long before they were first erected at Stonehenge, and suggests that they may have been used on another site at an earlier date. The belief that they were shipped out of Milford Haven, probably on sea-going rafts, is strengthened by the fact that two other foreign stones used at Stonehenge have been linked with micaceous sandstone from the vicinity of Llangwm and Mill Bay, Cosheston.

The only certain example of a stone circle in Pembrokeshire is Gors Fawr (SN 134294) which has sixteen stones, none taller than 3ft (1m), and two outlying standing stones, each over 5ft (1½m).

More common, but even less easy to explain, are the lone standing stones, of which over seventy have been identified. Excavations at Rhos y Clegyrn (SM 913355) and at the Devil's Quoit (SR 981950) on Stackpole Warren have produced evidence of ritual practice in the area surrounding the standing stone. Among the more impressive examples are Bedd Morus (SN 038365), Tymeini (SM 996377), Maen Dewi

St Govan's Chapel, wedged in the cliffs. St Govan is believed to have landed here from Ireland, and to have been buried beneath the altar (*Wales Tourist Board*)

Ffyst Samson, near St Nicholas. Samson was credited with lifting the capstone of the nearby cromlech (*John L. Jones*)

(SM 775274), Harold Stone, Haroldston West (SM 861147), Mabesgate (SM 827076), Sandy Haven (SM 848083), Harold Stone near Bosherston (SR 968959) and Harold Stone on Skomer Island. It was mistakenly believed that the stones marked King Harold's victories over the Welsh in 1063. Hangstone Davey (SM 895146) is said to be named after a sheep thief who rested against the stone, but was strangled when the sheep he carried roped round his neck struggled and slipped over the top of the stone.

Standing stones occasionally occur in pairs, as at Tafarn Bwlch (SN 083336), Cerrig Meibion Arthur (SN 118310) and Waun Lwyd (SN 157313). At Parc y Meirw (SM 998359) is a rare alignment of eight stones extending over 140ft (42m). The tallest is 8ft (2.5m) high but most of the stones are now prostrate or set in a roadside hedge-bank.

Evidence of occupation by the Bronze Age people is provided by the round barrows in which they buried their dead. The barrows, or cairns, are often sited on high ground, near ancient trackways. They may be seen along the prehistoric route that follows the summits of the Presely Hills, sometimes in groups, as at Foel Cwm Cerwyn (SN 095314). Moel Drygarn (SN 157336) derives its name from the three cairns on its summit, upon which was later built an Iron Age hill fort. A group of six barrows occupies Crugiau Cemais (SN 125416), beside the road from Nevern to Cardigan. In the south, barrows follow The Ridgeway westward from Tenby, with large groups at Dry Burrows (SM 948997) and Wallaston (SM 925003). The barrows mark the graves of those who succumbed while travelling along the trade routes from Wessex to Ireland, in pursuit of copper and gold.

The early Bronze Age people, who arrived around 1800BC, buried their dead singly, with beakers or food vessels, but those who arrived some 300 years later practised cremation and placed the ashes in urns that were buried beneath the barrows, sometimes accompanied by decorated 'pygmy cups' which appear to have served a particular ritual purpose. Examples of these vessels may be seen at the Tenby Museum.

The men who brought iron to replace bronze began to reach Pembrokeshire from about 500BC, and they have left their traces in the defensive settlements that are found on hill tops and on promontories around the coast.

The most outstanding hill forts occupy the summits of Moel Drygarn, Garn Fawr (SM 895388) and Carn Ingli (SN 062372). Hut sites are traceable both within and outside the dry-stone walls of the ramparts that surround the summits and it is likely that the settlements continued to be occupied up to around 500AD. On a smaller scale are hill forts situated on igneous outcrops, such as Great Treffgarne (SM 956250) and Carn Alw (SN 139337) which has, at its approach, a rare *chevaux-de-frise*, an area of stones set on end in the ground to protect it against attack, particularly by cavalry. Prominent sites in relatively low-lying areas were similarly defended, as at Castell Mawr (SN 118378), Caerau Gaer (SN 139161), Roman's Castle (SM 895106), Rudbaxton Rath (SM 986188), Bulliber (SR 902966) and Merrion (SR 940975). Occasionally the forts occupied hill slopes rather than summits. Some of these were defended by concentric rings of bank and ditch, as at Summerton Camp (SM 990301), Caerau, Moylegrove (SN 124454) and Castle Meherin (SN 147117). Others are distinguished by having enclosures adjacent to the main fortified area, as at Scollock Rath (SN 019242) and Lady's Gate Rath (SM 922232).

There are over fifty promontory forts recorded around the Pembrokeshire coast, and these include Penrallt Ceibwr (SN 111459), Castell Treruffydd (SN 100448), Castell Coch (SM 840338), Caerau, Abereiddi (SM 777307), Castell Heinif (SM 724247), Penpleidiau (SM 763240), Porth-y-rhaw (SM 787242), Black Point Rath (SM 860153), the Deer Park (SM 758090), Great Castle Head (SM 848060), Linney Head (SR 888957), Crocksydam (SR 935943) and Greenala Point (SS 007966). Clawdd y Milwyr, 'the warriors' dyke', on

St David's Head, has the remains of a settlement behind massive ramparts and, on the slopes above Porth Melgan, are traces of fields that were cultivated by the community resident there. Finds from the excavation of Clawdd y Milwyr are deposited at the Tenby Museum.

Headlands at the junction of steep-sided valleys were also defended in the manner of promontory forts, as at Castell Rhyd-y-brown (SN 067223), Llanddewi Gaer (SN 145160) and Capeston Rath (SM 868095).

The people who came to Pembrokeshire during the first millennium BC brought with them the Celtic culture that had dominated Europe for some centuries and a language that survives, in one of its derivative forms, as Welsh.

Pembrokeshire remained free of Roman occupation. Its people were described by Ptolemy in the second century AD as the *Demetae,* and their territory was known as *Demetia,* from which was derived Dyfed, the name of the Welsh kingdom that covered the south-western peninsula, west of Carmarthen. This name was recently revived as the title of the administrative county that amalgamated the former counties of Cardigan, Carmarthen and Pembroke as a result of the reorganisation of local government in 1974. The Demetae may have been a people that the Romans had no desire to tackle, or there may have been a compact made between them: the fact is that the Romans penetrated no further west than Carmarthen, and Demetia remained a distinctive cultural region more closely linked with Ireland than with the rest of Wales.

Even so there were Roman influences, evidence of which has been handed down in the remains of the small stone buildings set within rectangular enclosures, found at Ford, near Wolfscastle, Castle Flemish (SN 007267) and Trelissey (SN 174079), near Amroth. These were once considered to be Roman forts or military stations, but have been identified as native homesteads incorporating features found in Roman villas.

Some time during the fourth century AD, an Irish tribe known as the Deisi, from Deece in County Meath, came under their leader Eochaid Allmuir, and established an Irish dynasty that was to rule in Pembrokeshire for the next few centuries. It was during this period that writing first appears, inscribed on stone in a Goidelic form, known as ogham. The ogham alphabet consists of twenty characters made up of four groups of one to five lines, which indicates that it had a manual basis, and seems to have evolved in southern Ireland. The lines are cut on the edge, or arris, of a stone pillar, on either side or obliquely across it:

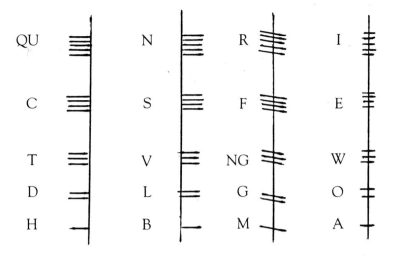

The inscriptions which date from the fifth and sixth centuries were often in Latin as well as in ogham, with the Goidelic filiation *maqi* corresponding to the Latin *fili*. A stone now forming a windowsill in the south transept of Nevern church is inscribed in Latin MAGLOCUNI FILI CLUTORI, (the stone of) Maglocunus son of Clutorius, and in ogham MAGLICUNAS MAQI CLUTARI. A stone pillar beside the church porch has VITALIANI EMERETO on its face in Latin and, along its left angle reading upwards, VITALIANI in ogham.

Later monuments, dating from the seventh to the ninth centuries, bear carved crosses, with no inscription. Then, belonging to the tenth and eleventh centuries, there are sculptured crosses, elaborately decorated and usually associated with ecclesiastical or monastic centres. The cross at Carew bears the inscription MARGITEUT REX ETG FILIUS, in memory of Maredudd son of Edwin who was killed in 1035. The inscriptions on the cross at Nevern have not been deciphered, although the one at the back of the cross is considered to be an abbreviated form of *dominus*. In the south transept in St David's Cathedral is a fractured pillar stone inscribed PONTIFICIS ABRAHAM FILII HIC HED (et) ISAC QUIESCUNT, commemorating Hedd and Isaac, the sons of Bishop Abraham who were killed during a Viking raid on the Cathedral in 1080.

Pembrokeshire lay in the path of the early Christian 'saints', or missionaries, in their ceaseless travelling between Ireland and the Continent, establishing ecclesiastical foundations, or *llanau*, which later developed as churches. The large number of place-names containing the name of the founder saint: Llanddewi, Llandeilo, Llanfyrnach and Llangolman are 'the churches of saints David, Teilo, Brynach and Colman'. Saint David had close on sixty dedications in south-west Wales, eight in Cornwall and seven in Brittany. His great monastic foundation at St David's developed as a 'mother church', ruled by a community or *clas* of canons serving under an abbot or bishop, all sharing the revenues of the church, and there were similar mother churches at St Dogmael's, Nevern, Llawhaden, Rhoscrowther, St Issell's and Penally.

From the middle of the ninth century, the churches suffered from incursions by Norsemen from settlements in Ireland. Although they probably established trading posts around the coast, there is no trace of permanent settlement and the only archaeological evidence is provided by a small leaden weight, with an embossed brass inset decorated by a Norse dragon, found on the foreshore at Freshwater West. They are remembered only in the names of coastal sites and islands and isolated rocks, such as Angle, Dale, Goultrop, Ramsey, Skokholm, Skomer, Emsger.

Following the death in 1093 of Rhys ap Tewdwr, the powerful prince of South Wales, the Normans were quick to invade the area. Roger de Montgomery, Earl of Shrewsbury, and his son Arnulf, marched across Wales and established a stronghold on a narrow promontory jutting into the Pembroke river, which they left in the care of Gerald de Windsor, who married Nest, 'the Helen of Wales' and daughter of Rhys ap Tewdwr. The former *cantref* of Penfro became a county palatine in 1138 and Gilbert de Clare was created Earl of Pembroke.

In north Pembrokeshire, Robert Fitzmartin occupied the stronghold of the Welsh chieftain at Nevern and established a Norman lordship in the former *cantref* of Cemais. The *cantref* of Pebidiog, in which St David's lay, had been granted by the Welsh princes to the see and was not invaded, but the Welsh bishops were replaced by Normans.

In accordance with their custom, the Normans built, or promoted the establishment of, a number of religious houses. Robert Fitzmartin brought monks from Tiron to set up an abbey at St Dogmael's. Monkton Priory, originally a cell of the Benedictine Abbey of Séez in Normandy, was a gift of Arnulf de Montgomery. Robert, son of Richard FitzTancred, founded an Augustinian Priory, the ruins of which stand on the banks of the Cleddau at Haverfordwest, and the Dominicans, or Black Friars, also had a house in that town.

Richard FitzTancred, descended from Flemish immigrants introduced by Henry I and given land in mid-Pembrokeshire in 1108, was in

Manorbier Castle, birthplace of Giraldus Cambrensis (Gerald of Wales) in 1147 (*Wales Tourist Board*)

occupation of Haverfordwest Castle when Giraldus Cambrensis visited the town in 1188, accompanying Archbishop Baldwin of Canterbury preaching the Third Crusade.

Giraldus was born at Manorbier Castle in 1146, a grandson of Gerald de Windsor and great-grandson of Rhys ap Tewdwr. He failed in his ambition to become Bishop of St David's, despite three visits to Rome to plead his case. In his writings, *Itinerary through Wales* and *Description of Wales,* he gave a lively and perceptive account of contemporary life. He died in 1223 and was buried at St David's.

Throughout the Norman period the Welsh continued to harass the invaders. In 1189, the Lord Rhys, freed from his compact with the Crown on the death of Henry II, occupied the southern part of Pembrokeshire, except for Pembroke. In 1215, his sons went into attack and were supported by Llywelyn the Great. Llywelyn the Last overran the Norman lordships in 1257 but failed to take Pembroke.

In 1405 Owain Glyn Dŵr came, with an army of 10,000 to meet 2,500 French mercenaries landed at Milford Haven and, with the combined force, attacked Haverfordwest and Tenby before marching victoriously through Wales and across Offa's Dyke to the borders of Worcester.

The prophecies of the Welsh poets appeared to have been fulfilled when at Pembroke Castle on 28 January 1457 a son was born to the fourteen-year-old Margaret Beaufort, Lancastrian heiress and widow of Edmund Tudor, Earl of Richmond. As descendant of Cadwaladr the Blessed, the last Welsh king of Britain, the boy Henry, it was foretold, would regain that throne and free his people from the English yoke.

In 1461 Pembroke was captured by the Yorkist, William, Lord Herbert, who took Henry into his care at Raglan Castle, and there he remained until Herbert's death nine years later. He then returned to Pembroke and, in 1471, following the battle of Tewkesbury, was taken to France by his uncle, Jasper, Earl of Pembroke, and given refuge in the Court of Brittany. On 1 August 1485, Henry set sail from Harfleur, with 2,000 French mercenaries, some Breton adventurers, Scots archers and 500 English exiles, and a week later landed at Mill Bay, near Dale. From there he marched through Haverfordwest and across the Presely Hills to Cardigan, and on to Bosworth Field, where he swiftly defeated King Richard III, and founded the Tudor dynasty.

The Tudor period produced men of eminence in Pembrokeshire amongst whom were Sir John Perrot, reputedly a natural son of Henry VIII, who became Lord Deputy of Ireland; Robert Recorde, who was the first to write books on mathematics in English; George Owen, author of *The Description of Penbrokshire*; and George William Griffith, the antiquary.

Sir Rhys ap Thomas, who had supported Henry at Bosworth, was made Chamberlain of South Wales and a Knight of the Garter, which honour he celebrated magnificently with a tournament at Carew Castle.

The monasteries in Pembrokeshire in the early sixteenth century were as ill endowed and undermanned as in the rest of Wales, and unable to fulfil their obligations. Without exception they fell within the terms of the Act of 1536 for the suppression of the smaller monasteries with incomes of less than £200 a year, but the friaries were not dissolved until 1538, and the Commandery of the Knights of St John of Jerusalem at Slebech was not appropriated until 1540.

Henry VIII's chief instrument in carrying out religious reform in West Wales was William Barlow who had been appointed Prior of

Haverfordwest by the Queen, Anne Boleyn, as Marchioness of Pembroke, in 1534. Two years later he was consecrated Bishop of St David's. His reforms made him so unpopular that he was denounced by the Chapter as a heretic. He failed to remove the see from St David's to Carmarthen but succeeded in transferring the bishop's residence to Abergwili and caused the ruin of the Bishop's Palace at St David's by stripping the lead from its roof. He surrendered Lamphey Palace to the King who leased it to Barlow's godson, Richard Devereux.

When Mary, on her accession in 1553, restored the Pope's authority, Barlow's successor as bishop, Robert Ferrar, was condemned to death and burned at the stake at Carmarthen. William Nichol, an unknown, achieved martyrdom at the stake in High Street, Haverfordwest on 9 April 1558.

Llangloffan Chapel, one of the earliest Baptist chapels in Wales

During the following century, despite repressive measures, religious dissent continued to rise and Nonconformity became a potent factor in the life of the people. The earliest congregation of dissenters in Pembrokeshire met, in 1638, at the Green Meeting, later to become the Albany Independent Chapel, at Haverfordwest. The Quakers had also established themselves at Haverfordwest in the early 1630s and had meeting houses at Redstone, Puncheston and elsewhere. Constant persecution led Lewis David of Llanddewi Velfrey to purchase 3,000 acres (1,200ha) of land in Pennsylvania from William Penn in 1681, where he and his fellows established settlements which they named Haverford and Narberth and which are by now suburbs of Philadelphia.

John Wesley visited Pembrokeshire in 1763, the first of fourteen visits during which he preached to congregations all over the county. His last visit, in 1790, at the age of eighty-eight, was undertaken only a few months before his death and is commemorated by a plaque outside the library at Haverfordwest. The Moravians formed a Society at Haverfordwest in 1755 and built a chapel on St Thomas's Green which was their only chapel in Wales until it was demolished in 1961.

Except for Pembroke and parts of the south, Pembrokeshire was for the King at the outbreak of the Civil War. In the summer of 1643 the Earl of Carbery, the Royalist commander, advanced into the county and was warmly received. The principal towns were garrisoned and castles and country houses were converted into Royalist strongholds. Plans for an assault on Pembroke were thwarted when Parliamentary ships had to seek shelter in the Haven and their presence assisted Major General Rowland Laugharne, who commanded the Cromwellian forces in Pembrokeshire, to disperse the Royalist garrison. Carbery was replaced by Sir Charles Gerard, an able professional soldier, who quickly re-established Royalist control, but before his task was complete he was summoned to Bristol to join Prince Rupert. Laugharne took advantage of his absence to recover his losses but Gerard returned early in 1645 and restored the Royalist position. Once more he was called away, following the King's defeat at Naseby and again Laugharne seized his opportunity. With a strong force from Pembroke and Tenby, he routed the King's men at the battle of Colby Moor, and captured Haverfordwest, Carew, Picton and Manorbier castles and brought the first Civil War to an end in Pembrokeshire.

The second Civil War was precipitated in Pembrokeshire. Laugharne, along with Colonel Rice Powell and John Poyer, the mayor of Pembroke, passed from their allegiance to Parliament to an open declaration for the King. Poyer refused to submit to Colonel Fleming who had been sent to replace him as governor of Pembroke Castle and eventually Cromwell arrived to suppress 'the Welsh insolence'. He laid siege to the castle but the garrison held out for forty-eight days and only surrendered when the Protector brought in heavy guns by sea. Laugharne, Powell and Poyer were tried by court-martial in London and sentenced to death but it was decreed that the death of one would satisfy justice. The lot fell on Poyer and he was executed at Covent Garden in April 1649.

Cromwell ordered the demolition of castles that he considered potentially dangerous but none was completely destroyed. William Walter complained that his castle at Roch had suffered damage and plunder to the value of £3,000 and went to London to advance his claim for compensation, taking with him his daughter, Lucy, who captivated Prince Charles Stuart, later King Charles II, and became the mother of his eldest illegitimate child, the Duke of Monmouth.

Although it is claimed that it was the vote of a Pembrokeshire member, Sir Arthur Owen of Orielton, that secured the Hanoverian succession in 1706, the Pembrokeshire gentry remained stoutly Jacobite and expressed their support by the formation, in 1725, of the Society of Sea Serjeants. The Society met at Tenby and other seaport towns in West Wales each year 'to spend a week together in innocent mirth and recreation', during which they feasted and drank 'to the King over the water' in glasses emblazoned with a dolphin within an eight-pointed star, which was their badge.

On 22 February 1797, at Carreg Wastad on the windswept coast of the Pencaer Peninsula, there came ashore an invading force consisting of 600 French regulars and 800 'abandoned rogues' released from the French gaols under the command of an Irish-American adventurer, William Tate, whose orders were to destroy Bristol or, if this were not possible, to land in Cardigan Bay and march on to Liverpool. Tate, who had established his headquarters at Trehowel Farm, was led to believe that a formidable army had gathered against him, while his own men, having plundered the well stocked larders and cellars of the surrounding farms, were in no condition to wage war. The defence, in fact, comprised the Castlemartin Troop of the recently formed Pembroke Yeomanry, the Pembroke Fencibles, the Cardiganshire Militia and 50 seamen from Milford Haven, totalling 750 rank and file, under the command of Lord Cawdor. The French, however, took the women who had assembled on the facing slopes at Fishguard, in their red shawls, to be grenadier reinforcements. Tate considered his position to be hopeless and agreed to an unconditional surrender. He delivered his sword to Lord Cawdor and signed articles of capitulation before leaving Trehowel under escort for Haverfordwest, while his men laid down their arms on Goodwick Sands. The last invasion of Britain had lasted less than forty-eight hours.

A monument in the churchyard on Fishguard Square commemorates Jemima Nicholas, 'the Welsh heroine', who marched against the invaders and brought back a dozen Frenchmen at the points of her pitchfork. The Pembroke Yeomanry was granted the right to wear 'Fishguard' on their standard and appointments, the only battle honour ever awarded for action fought on British soil.

The period of depression that followed the Napoleonic wars led to rural discontent that eventually manifested itself on the night of 13 May 1839 at Efailwen on the main road from Crymych to Narberth. A group of men dressed in women's clothes gathered there and destroyed a toll-gate that had lately been erected, and set fire to the toll-keeper's lodge. Thus began the Rebecca Riots, so named from the verse in the book of Genesis stating that the seed of Rebecca would 'possess the gates of those which hate them' or, according to local tradition, from Big Rebecca of Llangolman, the only woman whose clothes were large enough to fit Thomas Rees, 'Twm Carnabwth', the leader of the revolt. The riots spread and led, in time, to the introduction by the government of measures that eased the situation in the rural areas.

Agriculture, the traditional mainstay of Pembrokeshire for many centuries, gained a new proficiency with the introduction of new methods of crop rotation and animal husbandry, although progress was slow and there were periods of serious depression and of artificial prosperity. Since the last war, systems of farming have become vastly more efficient but there have been considerable fluctuations in production. Dairy farming showed a steady rise in milk yield until the recent imposition of milk quotas, and, while still important, the growing of early potatoes and turkey breeding have been substantially reduced.

In 1957, following the closure of the Suez Canal, the Government decided to develop a deep-water port at Milford Haven to receive the giant oil tankers that carried vast tonnages of crude oil round the Cape of Good Hope from the Middle East. Milford became the largest oil port in Britain, but the effect on the rest of the county was not great.

Much greater has been the impact of tourism. For the last two centuries, the popularity of Pembrokeshire as a place for holidays has grown steadily and, since the designation of the National Park, more and more people have been attracted by its unspoilt beauty and the provision for its enjoyment.

3
COTTAGE TO CASTLE, CHAPEL TO CATHEDRAL

Cottage, church and castle provide the main interest in Pembrokeshire for students of architecture. There never was an abundance of great stately homes, and although George Owen states that there were 'many mansion houses' in the county in the sixteenth century, most of these appear to have been modest country residences.

Cottages and Houses

The typical Pembrokeshire cottage was a single-storey building often limewashed in white, or in pastel shades of orange, pink, grey or a morning-glory blue. The walls were made of clom, a mixture of clay and chopped straw, and the roof was thatched with rushes or straw, or covered with local slate and grouted against wind and rain. The interior comprised a single room, often divided by a tall-backed settle or an oak dresser hung with jugs and patterned plates. Later, a thin board partition was erected to provide a bedroom, and often there was a narrow room running the length of the cottage at the rear. A ladder led to a low loft, lit by a skylight. A culm fire (see page 72) was kept burning day and night in *y simnai fawr*, a large inglenook, where the family passed the hours on wintry nights in story-telling and song, and young men fashioned bits of wood into intricately designed love-spoons.

The stone used in buildings reflected the geological features of the locality, for people used the material that was most ready to hand. Igneous rock provided much of the building stone in the northern area, except for places like Cilgerran and Abereiddi, where slate was more available, and St David's, where the cathedral was built of purple sandstone. Around Haverfordwest, the local mudstone was used, green micaceous sandstone at Neyland, red marls around Milford, and grey limestone in the south.

Giraldus Cambrensis noted, towards the end of the twelfth century, that the Welsh 'do not live together in towns or villages and fortresses. Rather after the manner of hermits, they cling to the edge of the forests where, instead of constructing permanent homes, they built cottages of woven twigs that last but for a year'. With the advent of the Normans, however, small civil communities were established in the vicinity of the castles, and in south Pembrokeshire there developed a scattering of nucleated villages.

By the end of the eighteenth century, as a result of enclosure, when there was considerable encroachment upon common land, the Pembrokeshire landscape had largely assumed its present patchwork appearance. In the upland areas, the practice of transhumance which derived from a pastoral nomadism, continued until the last century. Cattle, sheep and goats were taken from the *hendre,* the winter dwelling, for summer grazing on moorland pastures, where the family would reside in a *hafod,* or summer dwelling. Occasionally a *tŷ un-nos,* 'a one-night house', would appear on common land, erected in the belief that a bothy built and roofed between sundown and sunrise so that smoke appeared from its chimney at dawn would be the freehold property of its builder, together with an area of land measuring an axe-throw in each direction.

Penrhos Cottage (SN 102258), believed to have been built originally as a *tŷ un-nos* but reconstructed early in the nineteenth century, was purchased by the Pembrokeshire County Council in 1971 and is preserved as an example of a traditional Pembrokeshire cottage containing the furniture and fittings left by its last occupants, Rachel and Maria Williams.

The traditional farmhouse comprised a dwelling separated from the byre only by a cattle-feeding walk, and often with barn and stable added so that, on level ground, it would form one long building, while on a slope the separate parts would be stepped.

Medieval houses in Pembrokeshire had their primary accommodation on the first floor, usually over a vaulted undercroft in the manner depicted in the Bayeux Tapestry and still to be seen at the Bishop's

Palace at St David's and in the episcopal residences at Llawhaden and Lamphey, and at Monkton Old Hall. A fortified variation developed as a tower house, such as Eastington at Rhoscrowther, the Old Rectory at Angle, Bonville's Court near Saundersfoot, and the Old Rectory at Carew Cheriton.

An unusual feature of Pembrokeshire architecture is the tall, round chimneys, that are often misleadingly described as 'Flemish chimneys'. They appear in areas that were not settled by the Flemings and are more likely to derive from castle building. They are found in the Pembroke and Tenby district, with splendid examples at St Florence, and in a more squat and conical manner on the St David's peninsula, as at Rhoson (SM 729253) and Clegyr Boia (SM 737251), with an outlier at Garn, Llanychaer (SM 994348).

Although Pembrokeshire is unable to boast of many great stately homes today, it did have, at one time, houses of considerable consequence beside the castles like Carew, Llawhaden and Picton that had been converted into sumptuous residences. Haroldston House (SM 959146), outside Haverfordwest, the home of Sir John Perrot (1527–92), Lord Deputy of Ireland, was well appointed and stood 'surrounded by a pleasaunce and walled gardens', but is now a sad ruin, and the great house at Landshipping, splendidly refurbished in 1789, was never lived in again.

A number of houses stand on an early foundation. Orielton (SM 955992) is known to have been occupied by the Wyrriott family from the twelfth century to the sixteenth. It then passed by marriage to Sir Hugh Owen of Bodeon in Anglesey, the progenitor of a family that played a leading part in the history of the county for the next 300 years. The present house, which is the largest in Pembrokeshire, was built in 1743, but the fortunes of the Owen family were reversed, largely through profligacy and litigation; the estate was heavily mortgaged and, in 1857, had to be sold. It changed hands several times before it was purchased, in 1954, by the author and naturalist R. M. Lockley, who carried out studies of the habits of rabbits there which were published in his *Private Life of the Rabbit*, the book that inspired Richard Adams to write *Watership Down*. Orielton is now a Field Study Centre run by the Field Studies Council.

The fortified dwelling of Sir Elidyr de Stackpole, who flourished in the twelfth century, became the site of a castellated house that was, in turn, demolished by John Campbell, son of Alexander Campbell of Cawdor and his wife, Elizabeth Lort, the heiress of Stackpole. In 1735 he built an elegant double-fronted Georgian residence on the site,

which he embellished with fine furnishings and works of art, and surrounded by a deer park and 'pleasure grounds'. Among the treasures in
the house was the Hirlas Horn, a large drinking horn said to have been
given by Henry Tudor to Dafydd ab Ifan of Llwyndafydd in Cardiganshire in return to hospitality on his way to Bosworth. The house was
rased to the ground by Campbell's descendant in 1962 and the estate
became the property of the National Trust.

Slebech Park (SN 032139) was built in 1773 on the site of the Commandery of the Knights of St John of Jerusalem, established in the
twelfth century. After the dissolution of the monasteries it was purchased by Thomas Barlow and his brother, Roger, who had sailed in the
flagship of Sebastian Cabot on the Brazilian expedition of 1526.
Catherine Barlow became the wife of Sir William Hamilton and
brought with her an estate that included land at Hubberston upon
which Hamilton, and his nephew Charles Greville, established the
town of Milford.

Sealyham (SM 966280) stands on land granted to Thomas Tucker of
Cheshire for his services in the army of Edward III. From the Tuckers it
passed by marriage to John Owen Edwardes of Little Treffgarne, and it
was here that Captain Jack Edwardes bred the Sealyham terrier, recog-
nised as a separate breed in 1903. Of the same family was William
Edwardes, the first Lord Kensington, who built himself a castellated
mansion above St Bride's Haven on the site of a previous residence.

Boulston (SM 976128) was occupied by a cadet branch of the Wogan
family from around 1300 until it was purchased by Colonel Dudley
Ackland of Pennsylvania, who erected the present house in 1798.

George Owen, when describing the 'mansion houses' of north Pembrokeshire in 1603, frequently adds the information that they were
built 'about xxx years past', thus indicating the great amount of building or renovation that had taken place during the latter part of the
sixteenth century. Of his own important residence, as Lord of Cemais,
at Henllys (SN 107393), hardly a vestige remains, and the house has
long since been a farmhouse, like most of the other 'mansion houses'
mentioned. Court (SN 135394) at Eglwyswrw, the manor house of
David Martin, Bishop of St David's (1296–1328), has lost its
chamomile lawn but retains traces of its moat. Penybenglog (SN
113381), home of the antiquary George William Griffith and, later, of
Sir Watkin Lewes, who became Lord Mayor of London in 1780, has
only the merest hint of its former glory.

Llwyn-gwair (SN 073397), near Newport, was held by the Cole family in the fourteenth century, and from the fifteenth until the middle of

Lion Rock at Treffgarne, with the Presely Hills in the distance (*Roger Worsley*)

the present century by the Bowen family. It is now a country hotel.

A small Elizabethan house at Felindre Farchog (SN 101391), known as The College, was built by George Owen to provide education for the children and young people whose early lives, he noted with concern, were wasted in shepherding and herding cattle on the unenclosed lands of the neighbourhood. It bears the inscription *Llys Dŷ Arglwyddi Cemmes 1559–1620*, 'the court house of the lords of Cemais', where courts leet were held by the lord or his steward and attended by the residents of the district.

Ffynnone (SN 244386) was designed by John Nash in Doric style in 1793 and, although greatly altered in 1904, it is still one of the finest country houses in West Wales. Colby Lodge (SN 158082) was also built by Nash, and so was Sion House in Tenby, that was destroyed by fire in the 1930s. It is also claimed that he was responsible for building Temple Druid (SN 096272).

In 1799 the historian Richard Fenton built a residence surrounded by exotic shrubs in the shelter of the valley of the Gwaun, a little above Lower Fishguard, most of which he had inherited from his uncle, Samuel Fenton. He called it Plas Glynamel. Morgan Jones erected a Georgian house, with a *porte-cochère*, at Cilwendeg (SN 223388), with money he had obtained from the sale of the Skerries lighthouse, off Anglesey, in 1826. At about the same time, Charles Mathias, with a fortune that he had inherited from a German Moravian, built Lamphey Court in classical style, beside the ruins of Lamphey Palace. It is now a country hotel and restaurant.

Poyston (SM 969199) was the home of General Sir Thomas Picton, the hero of Waterloo, who was born at Haverfordwest in a house that is now the Dragon Hotel, in Hill Street, where many of the county families had their town residences.

Haverfordwest was the centre of the social scene in winter, when the gentry occupied their town houses so as to be able to attend the many parties and balls, to which the ladies were conveyed in sedan chairs.

Foley House, in Goat Street, was built by John Nash in 1794 for Richard Foley whose brother, Admiral Sir Thomas Foley, had served with Nelson at Cape St Vincent and Copenhagen. Nelson received the freedom of Haverfordwest here, during his visit to Milford in 1802. The house has been sadly disfigured on being renovated and adapted as offices for the County Council.

'The Blue Lagoon' at Abereiddi – a disused slate quarry flooded to provide a safe anchorage (*Roger Worsley*)

Tenby provided for the enjoyment of the summer season with the building of fine houses along the sea-front. Of its medieval houses only the Tudor Merchant's House and Plantagenet House remain.

Any shortcoming that Pembrokeshire may have in stately homes is more than compensated by the number, and diversity, of castles erected within its borders.

Castles

Pembrokeshire is the county of castles. To secure their occupation, the Normans found it necessary to construct fifty-one simple earthworks, either surmounted by a wooden palisade and timber buildings, as portrayed in the Bayeux Tapestry, or surrounded by a bank and ditch. In some cases, the timber building was replaced by a stone castle, of which sixteen survive, in lordly ruin or in human occupation.

In addition to the powers the Norman barons possessed as tenants-in-chief to the king, by virtue of their conquest with private arms they also assumed those of the defeated Welsh rulers, and this set them apart as marcher lords, or lords of the March, which stretched along the Welsh border and westward to Pembrokeshire.

The boundaries of the Norman lordships largely coincided with those of the former Welsh hundreds of Penfro, Arberth, Daugleddau, Rhos, Pebidiog and Cemais, and of the commot of Cilgerran which was the part of the hundred of Emlyn situated in Pembrokeshire.

After the Edwardian conquest of Wales in 1282, there was no longer the same need for castles and they soon fell into disrepair. Some were brought into use during the Wars of the Roses, and several were garrisoned during the Civil Wars. Seven of the castles are still occupied as private residences.

Pembroke Castle stands on a rocky promontory that may have been a fortified site in pre-Norman times. When Roger de Montgomery, Earl of Shrewsbury, and his son, Arnulf, invaded south Pembrokeshire in 1093 they erected 'a slender fortress of stakes and turf', but one that was sufficiently well defended to withstand an assault by the Welsh in the following year. In 1138 the castle was granted to Gilbert de Clare on being created Earl of Pembroke, but it was William Marshal who inherited the earldom, by marriage to Gilbert's grand-daughter, and who built the great keep and the towers that made Pembroke one of the most impregnable fortresses in Britain.

The Tudor Merchant's House at Tenby (*Countryside Commission*)

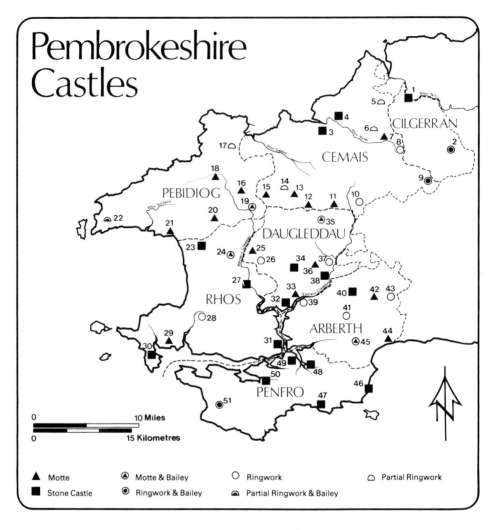

Pembrokeshire Castles

CILGERRAN

CEMAIS

PEBIDIOG

DAUGLEDDAU

RHOS

ARBERTH

PENFRO

0   10 Miles

0   15 Kilometres

▲ Motte   ◉ Motte & Bailey   ○ Ringwork   ⌒ Partial Ringwork

■ Stone Castle   ◉ Ringwork & Bailey   ⌒ Partial Ringwork & Bailey

1 Cilgerran	14 Puncheston	27 Haverfordwest	40 Narberth
2 Castell Crychydd	15 Little Newcastle	28 Walwyn's Castle	41 Sentence Castle
3 Newport	16 Letterston	29 St Ishmael's	42 Green Castle
4 Nevern	17 Castell Fartin	30 Dale	43 Castell Cynon
5 Pen-yr-allt	18 Castle Morris	31 Benton	44 Amroth
6 Eglwyswrw	19 Wolfscastle	32 Picton Castle	45 Begelly
7 Llain-fawr	20 Hayscastle	33 Picton Motte	46 Tenby
8 Dyffryn Mawr	21 Poyntz Castle	34 Wiston	47 Manorbier
9 Llanfyrnach	22 St David's	35 New Moat	48 Carew
10 Pengawsai	23 Roch	36 Dingstopple	49 Upton
11 Maenclochog	24 Camrose	37 Drim	50 Pembroke
12 Henry's Moat	25 Rudbaxton Motte	38 Llawhaden	51 Castlemartin
13 Castlebythe	26 Rudbaxton Rath	39 Minwear	

The stone castles are described on pp55-62

In 1452 Henry VI granted the earldom to his half-brother, Jasper Tudor and he took the young widow of his brother, Edmund, Earl of Richmond, to the castle to give birth, in 1457, to her son Henry, who was to become, as Henry VII, the founder of the Tudor dynasty. The castle was the chief stronghold of the Parliamentary forces during the Civil Wars.

The entrance, through the Barbican Gate, leads to the outer ward, and immediately to the left is the tower that is believed to have been the birthplace of Henry Tudor. The whole area is dominated by the massive donjon that rises to a height of 75ft (23m) and was probably the first completed portion of the castle. Beneath the inner ward lies a huge cavern, known as The Wogan, which gave access to the tidal Pembroke River.

The Pembroke town walls, of which sections are still standing, sprang from the Northgate Tower and from the Westgate Tower.

The castle is open to the public.

Carew Castle was established by Gerald de Windsor, custodian of Pembroke Castle, and was occupied by his descendants, the Carews, until about 1480, when Sir Edmund Carew sold it to Sir Rhys ap Thomas, who held a great tournament there in 1507 to celebrate his appointment as Knight of the Garter. In 1558 it was granted to Sir John Perrot who built the north wing, hoping to entertain Queen Elizabeth: instead, he was accused of treason and died in the Tower of London, leaving unfinished the long chambers with their mullioned windows gazing vacantly over the tidal estuary. The east wing, in which the gatehouse stands, is thirteenth century and contains a small hall and the chapel. The Great Hall, which occupies most of the west wing, was completed early in the fourteenth century. After the Civil War, the castle reverted to the Crowcombe branch of the Carew family whose descendant placed it in the care of the National Park Authority in 1983.

Upton Castle (SN 021047) was built in the thirteenth century as a minor stronghold on a creek of the Carew river, and is a private residence. In 1976 the National Park Authority entered into a management agreement of the castle grounds with the present owners and these are now open to the public. Some 250 species of trees and shrubs present an impressive sight, particularly in springtime. A small chapel adjoining the castle contains tombs of the Malefant family, the original owners.

Manorbier Castle is the birthplace of Giraldus Cambrensis, the celebrated twelfth-century historian. In 1185 he accompanied Prince

Carew Castle, scene of Sir Rhys ap Thomas's tournament of 1507 (*Wales Tourist Board*)

John to Ireland and, three years later, travelled through Wales with Archbishop Baldwin of Canterbury, preaching the Third Crusade, and wrote vivid contemporary accounts of conditions in the two countries. In 1670 the castle was purchased by Sir Erasmus Philipps of Picton Castle whose descendant is the present owner.

The roughly rectangular ward has a guard room, circular towers on either side of the gatehouse at the extremities, a chapel and a hall block at the far end. There is a private residence within the ward but the castle is open to the public.

Tenby Castle stands on the site of a stronghold described by a Welsh poet of the ninth century as 'a fine fortress above the sea'. The fragmentary remains include a barbican and a double tower of the early thirteenth century. Its ruin stands on an open space to which there is free access. The Tenby Museum was built partly within the castle walls, in 1878.

Narberth Castle (SN 110144) was captured by the Welsh in 1116 and on three other occasions during the following century, and was burned to the ground, probably accidentally, in 1299. It was 'decayed and wasted' by 1590, but a description given in 1539 states that the castle buildings formed a quadrant court approached by a gate on the north side, between the north-west tower and the Great Tower; that the kitchen, with the Great Hall over it, occupied the south end of the court, and that there was a bakehouse in the south-east tower, with a chapel above it. The west curtain had a gallery and a semi-circular tower and, along the eastern curtain, the Great Chamber stood above a vaulted pantry and cellar. The castle is in private ownership.

Llawhaden Castle (SN 074175) was probably built by Bernard, the first Norman bishop, elected to the see of St David's in 1115. Giraldus Cambrensis visited his uncle, Bishop David Fitzgerald, there in 1175. It was destroyed by the Lord Rhys in 1192. During the episcopacy of Bishop David Martin (1293–1327) the castle was transformed into a sumptuous fortified residence, with quarters for a garrison and a guesthouse. A causeway across the moat leads to the gatehouse, facing which, across the courtyard, was the Great Hall and the bishop's private quarters. The castle has been restored and is open to the public.

Wiston Castle (SN 022180) was built by Wizo, a leading Flemish immigrant who settled in the area around 1108. It was captured by the Welsh in 1147 and again in 1193, and was utterly destroyed by Llywelyn the Great in 1220, but was later rebuilt by William Marshal, Earl of Pembroke. Its shell keep, the only one in Pembrokeshire, surmounts a mound in a bean-shaped bailey. It is privately owned.

Picton Castle (SN 009135) stands to the west of an earlier motte. The present castle was built by Sir John Wogan, inspired by the layout of thirteenth-century castles he had seen while serving as Justiciary of Ireland between 1295 and 1313. It has drum towers, of unequal size, at each corner of a rectangular block to which a large four-storey addition was made by Sir Richard Philipps, the first Lord Milford, in about 1800. The castle has been extensively restored by the present owner, who is a descendant of the Philipps family. It is in private occupation, but the gardens are open to the public, and so is the Graham Sutherland Gallery which is situated in the courtyard of the castle.

Haverfordwest Castle was built on a spur overlooking the Western Cleddau and guarding its lowest fording point. It is believed to have been erected by Gilbert de Clare, afterwards the first Earl of Pembroke, around 1120, but there may well have been an earlier fortress on such a commanding site. The first record is of a visit by Giraldus Cambrensis in 1188, when the castle was occupied by Richard the son of Tancred, a Flemish settler. Richard's son was expelled by King John when he

Haverfordwest Castle by night (*B. R. Munt*)

passed through Haverfordwest on his way to Ireland in 1210, and the castle was granted to William Marshal, Earl of Pembroke. In 1218, when Llywelyn the Great set fire to the town, the castle survived, and it also withstood an attack by Owain Glyn Dŵr and his French mercenaries, newly landed in Milford Haven, in 1405.

At the outbreak of the Civil War it was garrisoned for the Parliament but it changed hands more than once and, in 1648, Cromwell ordered its destruction. The Mayor agreed to do so, provided the Protector would send him 'a competent quantity of powder', but the substantial remains indicate that he did not put his heart into the task. These include the walls of the Great Chamber, along the east wall, together with the solar, chapel and Great Hall. A gaol was built within the inner ward in 1779, and was later replaced by a three-storey building in the outer ward, which was used as a police headquarters until 1933. The building now houses the Castle Museum and the Record Office.

Benton Castle (SN 006069) is believed to have been built by Bishop Bek of St David's in the thirteenth century. Its three-storey tower, surmounted by an octagonal battlement, and the adjoining buildings, were ruined for several centuries until they were rebuilt in the 1930s. It is a private residence.

Dale Castle (SM 804058) may stand on the site of an earlier castle established by Richard de Vale, lord of Dale, in the twelfth century. It came into the hands of the Walter family early in the seventeenth century and was sold, in 1669, by Richard Walter, brother of Lucy, mistress of Charles II and mother of the Duke of Monmouth. It eventually passed to the Lloyd-Philipps family, in which it remains as a private residence.

Roch Castle (SM 880211) has a semi-circular tower with projecting chambers set on a rhyolitic rock, from which it takes its name. It was built, in the thirteenth century, by Adam de la Roche, and was purchased, in 1601, by William Walter, ancestor of Lucy Walter. In 1899 it was purchased by John Wynford Philipps, later Viscount St David's, and sold by his son in 1954. It is a private residence.

In north Pembrokeshire the Welsh hundred of Cemais was invaded by Robert Fitzmartin who occupied the native stronghold at Nevern (SN 083402). His grandson, William Martin, married a daughter of the Lord Rhys but he was driven out of Nevern, in 1191, by his father-in-law who, in turn, was imprisoned in the castle by his own sons. The castle stands above a ravine and has a high motte at the north-west angle of its bailey, the east angle point of which is isolated by a rock-cut ditch, leaving a platform upon which are the scant remains of a square keep that may have been built by the Lord Rhys.

Newport Castle (SN 057388) was built by William Martin, lord of Cemais, after he had been driven out of Nevern in 1191. It was captured by Llywelyn the Great in 1215 and suffered during Owain Glyn Dŵr's rebellion in 1405. From the Martins it passed by marriage to the Audleys of Heleigh, in Staffordshire. In 1497 James, Lord Audley was beheaded for treason and his estates became forfeit to the Crown, but Newport was restored to his son in 1534. The castle, and the lordship of Cemais, were then purchased by William Owen of Henllys, whose son was George Owen, the historian. The castle remains are of the thirteenth century: it comprised three towers and a gatehouse that stood between two flanking towers, one of which was demolished when a part was converted into a residence in 1859 by Sir Thomas Lloyd, to whom the castle had passed by marriage. His descendant is the present owner.

Cilgerran Castle (SN 195433) may have been established by Roger de Montgomery during his advance on Pembroke in 1093. It was held by Gerald de Windsor, custodian of Pembroke, at the beginning of the twelfth century. In 1164 it was captured by the Lord Rhys, and was taken and retaken before it was finally recovered by William Marshal the Younger, Earl of Pembroke, in 1223. He rebuilt the castle in locally quarried slate, erecting two drum towers astride the curtain wall, and a gatehouse with a double portcullis to guard the inner ward, inside which are the remains of a limekiln, kitchen and the north-west tower. The castle was granted by Henry VII to William Vaughan and it later passed to the Pryce family of Gogerddan. In 1938 it was purchased by Mrs Colby of Ffynnone who presented it to the National Trust. It is open to the public.

Churches

Once the Normans had consolidated their position by building castles, they lost no time in establishing ecclesiastic foundations.

At Pembroke, the church of St Nicholas, described as 'within the castle' but situated across the tidal inlet at Monkton, was presented by Arnulf de Montgomery, in 1098, to the Benedictine Abbey of Sèez in Normandy, along with twenty carucates of land, and was established as a priory, known as the Priory of Pembroke. It came under the patronage of the Earls of Pembroke, although it fell into the hands of the Crown for periods and, during the latter part of the fifteenth century, it was a cell of St Alban's Abbey. At the dissolution of the monasteries it was granted to John Vaughan and his wife Catherine, and soon fell into decay. In 1887 the church was restored and the choir of the Priory became the chancel and sanctuary. There are memorials to members of the Owen family of Orielton, and the tomb of Sir Francis Meyrick, who died in 1603.

Soon after Robert Fitzmartin had occupied Cemais, he visited the Abbey of Tiron, near Chartres in 1115, and returned with twelve monks, of a strict Benedictine Order, to establish the monastery at St Dogmael's, probably on the site of a Celtic house that had suffered at the hands of Norse marauders in 987. He endowed it with lands in Devon and in Ireland and raised it to the status of an abbey to which the Priories at Caldey and at Pill, near Milford, became subordinates. When the Abbey was suppressed in 1536, it was purchased by John

Bradshaw of Presteign. The remains of the extensive range of buildings include those of the Abbey church, cloisters, presbytery and infirmary, dating from the twelfth century onward.

Pill Priory was founded about 1170 by Adam de la Roche. Its monks were of the reformed Benedictine Order from Tiron like those of St Dogmael's. Llywelyn the Great pitched his camp here in 1220, before he set fire to Haverfordwest. A visit by the Bishop of St David's in 1405 revealed certain scandals and abuses. The Priory was granted to Sir Thomas Jones of Haroldston at the dissolution of the monasteries and was later exchanged by his stepson, Sir John Perrot, for lands at the Haverfordwest Priory. The impressive chancel arch is about all that remains of the Priory.

The Augustinian Priory, adjoining Freemen's Way at Haverfordwest, is believed to have been founded by Robert FitzTancred about 1200. It was dedicated to St Mary the Virgin and St Thomas the Martyr and was endowed with a number of advowsons and tithes within the barony of Haverford. In 1534 William Barlow was appointed Prior by Anne Boleyn as Marchioness of Pembroke, and soon afterwards became the controversial Bishop of St David's. The remains include those of a cruciform church with a central tower.

The Dominicans, or Black Friars, established a friary further up on the banks of the Cleddau, behind Bridge Street, which they dedicated to St Saviour. When it was dissolved, it became the property of Roger Barlow of Slebech, along with the Augustinian Priory.

The Knights of St John of Jerusalem founded a Commandery at Slebech during the twelfth century, and were granted lands in various parts of Pembrokeshire. At the dissolution, it was purchased by Roger Barlow and his brother, Thomas. Within the walls of its church, now ruinous, was buried Sir William Hamilton, beside his first wife, Catherine Barlow. The Order of St John hold a service there annually on the Sunday nearest to the Feast of St John.

A Preceptory of the Knights Templars was established at Templeton which, when the Templars were suppressed in 1308, was transferred to the Knights of St John at Slebech.

St David and his Cathedral

Pembrokeshire, from prehistoric time, has been on the crossroads of the western seaways, and the early Christian missionaries, or 'saints', took full advantage of its situation in their constant journeyings between Ireland and the Continent. In order to avoid the perilous seas

Whitesand Bay (near St David's) where St Patrick is said to have embarked for Ireland (*Wales Tourist Board*)

of the promontories, they followed a trans-peninsular route, and made the creeks and bays of the St David's peninsula their points of landing or departure. Legend is strong that St Patrick himself set sail from Whitesand Bay. St David's is the meeting point of a number of roads that come from the little coastal chapels where the Celtic saints offered prayers, or thanksgiving, for a safe voyage across the Irish Sea: Capel Padrig at Whitesand Bay, St Justinian at Porthstinan, Capel y Pistyll at Porth Clais, and St Non's Chapel. Other chapels connected by road with St David's were: Capel Cwmwdig, Capel y Gwrhyd, Capel yr Hen Fynwent and Whitewell Chapel.

One approaches St David's across a plateau that is broken only by a series of monadnocks: Carn Llidi, Carn Lleithr and Penberi. There is no indication that somewhere on this windswept peninsula lies the great cathedral church of the patron saint of Wales. Then, suddenly, one enters a village, that calls itself a city, the smallest in Britain, and it is only when one is halfway down its street, that a square tower, in plum-coloured stone, peeps out of the depths of the valley of the river Alun. Here David built his house of worship.

Little is known of his life. The earliest reference to him appears on a stone, at Llanddewi Brefi Church in Ceredigion, inscribed to the memory of Idnert son of Jacob 'who was killed while defending the church of the holy David from despoilation'. It dates from the early seventh century, not long after the death of David. A century or so later, the Irish *Martyrology of Tallaght* notes that the feast day of David was the first day of March, and there are written references to him in *The Catalogue of the Saints of Ireland* and in *The Martyrology of Oengus the Culdee*. Gourmonoc, a monk in the Abbey of Landévennec in Brittany referred to him, in 884, as *Aquaticus*, because he drank only water with his diet of bread and vegetables. Nine years later, Asser, the confidant of King Alfred, speaks of the monastery of the holy Dewi at St David's. In about 1095, *Vita Davidis*, the life of David, was written by Rhygyfarch, the son of Sulien, founder of the monastic school at Llanbadarn, near Aberystwyth, and, before that, twice bishop of St David's. It is from this *Vita* that we learn most of what is known about David.

He was the son of Sant, son of Cedig, son of Ceredig, the eponymous lord of Ceredigion, whose wife was a daughter of the Irish king, Brychan of Brecknock, and whose father was Cunedda Wledig, who had come south from Manaw Gododdin, on the Firth of Forth, at the end of the fourth century, to expel the Irish from North Wales. His mother was a nun named Non, who also had a Irish ancestry. He was baptised by Ailbe, or Elvis, of Munster, who had landed at Porth Clais, where a baptismal spring Ffynnon Dewi, suddenly appeared where there was none before. He was educated at the monastery of Hen Fynyw, near Aberaeron, and he also studied under Paulinus in north Carmarthenshire.

He is said to have established his religious house, in the first instance, at Tŷ Gwyn, under Carn Llidi, 'the cairn of the monastery'. When he wanted to move, for greater safety, to a less conspicuous site, he encountered the opposition of Boia, an Irish settler whose stronghold was at Clegyr Boia (SM 738252). In the end, he succeeded in siting his monastery in Glyn Rhosin, where the cathedral now stands.

Glyn Rhosin, and its Latin form *Vallis rosina*, means 'a bosky valley', and corresponds to the Irish reference to David as of *Cill Muine*, 'the cell in the thicket'; where *muine* is the same word as the Welsh *Mynyw* and Latin *Menevia*.

That David's reputation was widespread is proved by the dedications to him, which number more than sixty in South Wales, along with nine in the south-west of England and six in Brittany. His fame undoubtedly spread after the Synod of Brefi, summoned to denounce the Pelagian heresy. Pelagius was an Irishman who denied the doctrine of original sin and the synod had been called at Llanddewi Brefi because it was feared that the heresy was spreading in West Wales. Such was the multitude that had gathered, including princes, priests and peasants, that David could not be seen, until the ground miraculously rose under his feet. He was then seen and heard by all, and Pelagianism was driven out of the land.

David died on the first day of March, but the year of his death is uncertain and is commonly held to be 589. He was canonised by Pope Calixtus II in 1120 and, in 1389, the Archbishop of Canterbury ordered that his feast day should be celebrated. His shrine was sufficiently well known for William the Conqueror to visit it in 1081, although William's primary interest was more likely to be the reaching of an agreement with Rhys ap Tewdwr, the powerful prince of South Wales. Its importance may be gauged from the decree that two pilgrimages to St David's equalled one to Rome.

The original monastic settlement consisted of a group of wattle-and-daub huts and a small church, surrounded by a defensive earthwork. It is not known to what extent it would have grown before the Normans came, except that it was sufficiently wealthy for the Norsemen to raid it on ten occasions, during which two of its bishops were killed.

The cathedral was built by Bishop Peter de Leia (1176–98), much as the large cruciform church that remains today, except that it ended at the sanctuary wall, behind the high altar, and had a squat tower. The tower collapsed in 1220, destroying the presbytery, and was rebuilt on three pointed arches, retaining the round-headed western arch which had remained intact. The presbytery was rebuilt in the Early English style. Some further damage was caused by an earth tremor in 1248.

The building was extended eastward by Bishop David Martin (1296–1328) who built the Lady Chapel, leaving a small courtyard between it and the sanctuary. Bishop Gower (1328–47) heightened the aisle walls, introduced large tracery windows, and added two storeys to St Thomas à Becket's Chapel, and a second stage to the tower. He erected the south porch and vaulted the Lady Chapel, and built the splendid pulpitum, or screen, with provision for his own tomb on its south side.

The failure of the Norman builders to secure a firm foundation caused the northern arcading to lean outwards and in about 1400 flying buttresses were placed against the north wall to prevent the nave collapsing. The presbytery was re-roofed a century later, and its walls

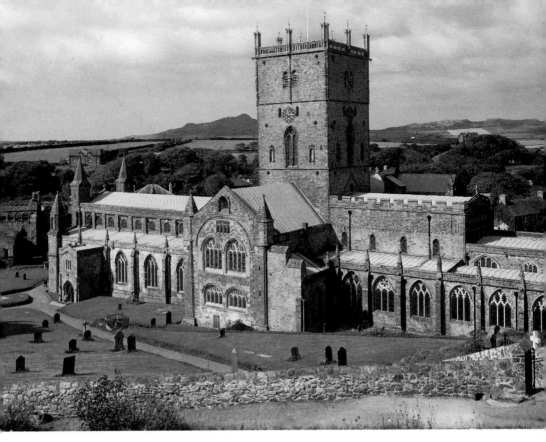

St David's Cathedral (*Countryside Commission*)

raised to allow for a lower pitched roof: the mark of the old pitch is to be seen on the tower.

The canons' stalls and the bishop's throne also date from about 1500. They range along three sides of the choir, while the fourth side has an open parclose screen separating it from the presbytery. The craftsmen who carved some of the misericords appear to have had a lively sense of humour. Of the twenty-eight stalls, six are cursal prebends, marked *P Cursalis*, which means that the canons occupying them obtained their income from various sources, whereas the other stalls had prebendal property. The first cursal prebend was held by the Master of St Mary's College, adjoining the Cathedral. At the dissolution it passed to the Crown but the stall, which has the royal coat of arms above it, was never occupied by a sovereign until the Queen visited the Cathedral in 1955. The last previous visit by a monarch was by Edward I in 1284.

The oak ceiling of the nave, with its decorative pendants, is a unique and memorable feature of the cathedral, and is attributed to Owen Pole, Treasurer (1472–1509).

Bishop Edward Vaughan (1509–23) added the third stage to the tower and converted the space between the back wall of the sanctuary and the Lady Chapel into a chapel, with fan-vaulted ceiling and a Perpendicular screen, dedicated to the Holy Trinity.

St David's narrowly escaped disaster when Bishop William Barlow (1536–68) attempted to remove the see to Carmarthen, but succeeded only in transferring the bishop's residence to Abergwili. And although it suffered less than many other cathedrals, the holy relics disappeared and the chantries were abolished, so that their chapels became roofless. The Cathedral suffered again during the Civil War, when the Cromwellians stripped lead from the roofs and smashed the glass in the windows.

During the succeeding centuries, the chapter had to struggle hard to maintain the fabric of the cathedral. The west front became dilapidated and was restored in 1793 to a controversial design by John Nash. In 1862 Sir Gilbert Scott began a wide-ranging restoration that took fifteen years to complete. He strengthened the tower and reconstructed its west arch, and rebuilt the west front on the lines of the original design, but retaining remnants of Nash's circular window to show, it is said, how out of place it was. The Lady Chapel was given a new vaulting in 1906 and restoration work has continued throughout the present century with the most excellent results.

The cathedral is normally entered through the south porch, built by Bishop Gower (1328–47), the inner doorway of which is highly ornamented. The archway is decorated with the Tree of Jesse, and there is a figure of St David in a niche in the western wall of the porch.

The floor of the nave slopes upwards steeply, so that it is 14ft (4.25m) higher at the east end of the Lady Chapel than it is at the west door. The clustered columns reach outward as they support massive, round arches, above which is another arcade that is divided into a triforium and clerestory. Over all is the ornamented ceiling carved of Irish and Welsh oak. There are traces of frescoes on three of the pillars, blurred by whitewash and its subsequent removal. The pulpitum, or rood screen, is beautifully ornate and of an unusual design built by Bishop Gower, whose tomb it holds at its south end. Beneath an arch nearby is the tomb of Bishop Morgan (1496–1505), finely carved in Bath stone.

The south transept was once used as the parish church but now it holds the Clergy's Vestry behind a wooden screen, which also partly hides a list of bishops on painted tiles. A portable altar stone, said to have been brought from Jerusalem by St David, is sunk into a small table, and an inscribed stone commemorates Hedd and Isaac, the sons of Bishop Abraham, who were killed during a Norse raid in 1078.

In the south choir aisle are tombs reported to be those of Rhys ap Gruffydd, otherwise known as the Lord Rhys, who died in 1197 (although the armour is that of a fourteenth-century knight), of Giraldus Cambrensis (1146–1223), and of Silvester the Physician whose 'dissolution showeth that medicine withstandeth not death'. In the southern bay are the tombs of Bishop Gervase (1215–29) and Bishop Anselm la Gras (1231–47).

The choir, with its canons' stalls, is beneath the tower, the ceiling of which is richly painted with episcopal coats of arms.

The floor of the presbytery largely consists of fifteenth-century encaustic tiles bearing the arms of Beauchamp, Berkeley and Edward III, and the Tudor rose.

The shrine of St David was built on the northern side of the presbytery about 1275. The high altar is modern and stands clear of the wall. The oak Perpendicular sedilia are fifteenth century. Before the high altar stands the table tomb of Edmund Tudor, Earl of Richmond, the father of Henry VII, whose body was transferred from the Greyfriars at Carmarthen by command of his grandson, Henry VIII, at the dissolution.

Holy Trinity Chapel lies behind the presbytery and has a fine fan-vaulting erected by Bishop Vaughan. His tomb is a large marble slab that lies before the altar and there is a modern statue of him, and another of Giraldus Cambrensis, standing in sixteenth-century niches. The altar is made up of pieces of inscribed stones, and the reredos comprises fourteenth-century panels.

In the recess, facing the altar, is an oaken casket bearing the holy relics. Near here at the Reformation they were hidden until they were found by Sir Gilbert Scott during the restoration of the cathedral. They are now placed, within the casket, in a jewelled reliquary presented by dignitaries of the Orthodox Church when they visited St David's in 1925, on the sixteenth centenary of the Council of Nicea.

At the end of the south choir aisle is the Chapel of St Edward the Confessor which was restored by the Viscountess Maidstone, who died in 1923, in memory of her grandfather, Bishop Jenkinson (1825–40). The elaborately carved alabaster tomb bears her effigy. A glass case contains the robes worn by the bishop at the coronation of Queen Victoria.

The Lady Chapel, which was built by Bishop Martin (1296–1328) has sedilia, and recesses that were built by Bishop Gower for his predecessors, Bishops Bek and Martin. A monument for Bishop John

Owen, who died in 1926, has been placed in Bishop Bek's recess. The vaulted roof was erected at the beginning of the present century to replace one that collapsed in 1775.

In St Nicholas' Chapel, at the end of the north choir aisle, there is a chantry founded in the early fourteenth century by Sir John Wogan, Chief Justice of Ireland, in which his tomb is reputed to lie. The chapel was restored in 1910 in memory of Dean Howell, who is buried in the eastern end.

The shrine of St David backs on to the north choir aisle. The tomb is said to be that of Rhys Gryg, 'hoarse Rhys', the son of the Lord Rhys.

The north transept is furnished as the County of Pembroke War Memorial to those who fell in the last war. Against the south wall is the shrine of St Caradoc, a twelfth-century hermit who lived near Haverfordwest, and there is a memorial to Thomas Tomkins, the seventeenth-century composer, who was born at St David's, where his father was the cathedral organist.

The Chapel of St Thomas à Becket was dedicated to that saint about 1220 and was refurnished in memory of Bishop Prosser in 1958. A new stained-glass window above the altar represents the saint and his murderers, and bears the arms of Henry II. A handsome Early English double piscina is placed in the south wall. The cathedral library, above St Thomas's Chapel, is open to the public on certain days.

The north aisle leads down to the west end of the Cathedral where there are several inscribed stones, most bearing crosses, found in the neighbourhood, and a pre-Reformation bell. The font may be pre-Norman, on a thirteenth-century base, and near it is another font which is said to be one of the cathedral's oldest relics.

A door in the north aisle opens on to all that remains of the cloisters that provided a covered way from the Cathedral to St Mary's College. The college was founded in 1377 by Bishop Adam Houghton, and John of Gaunt and his wife, who had perceived that 'the Service of God was ill-performed in the Cathedral of St David's, and because there were few priests that could sing well, founded a Chapel or Chauntry of one master and seven priests who were to reside there continually and serve God'. The college chapel was restored and converted in 1966 as the cathedral hall.

The growing popularity of St David's as a place of pilgrimage called for the provision of accommodation for pilgrims. Bishop David Fitzgerald had experienced difficulty, as well as a financial strain, in providing adequately for the entertainment of Henry II in 1172, and the visit of Edward I and Queen Eleanor in November 1284 may well have emphasised the lack of facilities available to the bishop in extending the customary hospitality. The remains of the western range, and the northern wall of the courtyard of the Bishop's Palace, indicate that there was a building on the site in the twelfth century.

The magnificent ruin that stands across the River Alun from the cathedral, with its elegant arcaded parapet chequered in white spar and purple sandstone so as to give it a Moorish appearance, is attributed to Bishop Gower, although in fact he built only about a half of it. The gatehouse, the bishop's hall and solar, and the chapel in the north-west corner of the courtyard, had already been built by Bishop Bek towards the end of the thirteenth century, and any unfinished work is likely to have been completed by Bishop David Martin.

It was Bishop Gower, Bishop Martin's successor, who had the vision of grandeur. Not satisfied with the bishop's hall, he built the more massive great hall, with its elaborately decorated porch and rose window, and he erected the arcaded parapet above his own work and the work of others alike. He probably began building the bishop's chapel, to the immediate left of the gate, the kitchen and a passage giving access to the two halls. A wing leading off the solar was added in the sixteenth century, probably by Bishop Vaughan (1509–22) in order to provide a more spacious private apartment. An indication of the spaciousness of the Bishop's Palace is provided by the innocent boast that all the bishops of Europe could dine together within its walls.

The Cathedral Close was surrounded by a wall, broken by four gates, of which only Porth-y-twr, 'the tower gateway', survives. Its octagonal tower was restored in 1930 to its former use as the Cathedral belfry. Porth Padrig lay below the Deanery and led to the cathedral from the south; Porth Gwyn stood on the hill to the west of the Bishop's Palace, and Porth Boning, near the Canonry, gave access from the north.

The wall was built during the latter part of the thirteenth century by Bishop Bek, and may be seen in its full height along the south side of the close. In 1379 the wall and the gates were reported to be in ruins and ordered to be repaired, and it would appear that the present remains are largely the result of this renovation.

No place in Britain has a longer unbroken history of religious settlement than St David's, in its hidden valley in the westernmost part of Wales. For close on fifteen centuries there have been those who by their pilgrimage have made Tŷ Ddewi, the house of David, one of the great centres of Christendom, comparable with Canterbury and Compostela.

4
PEMBROKESHIRE AT WORK

Industry

Though rural and remote, Pembrokeshire has not been without its in-dustries. Not so long ago, there was a thriving coalfield producing some of the finest anthracite in the world, and there was also mining, though on a far lesser scale, for copper, iron and manganese ores, for silver lead and even for gold. Granite was quarried for building and road-making, and slate for roofing lowly cottages and palaces in distant places. There were corn mills, woollen mills and paper mills, tanneries and turneries, iron works, rope works and churn works, and there were small cottage industries producing everyday requirements, from clogs to coracles, and most of them survived into the present century. There was ship-building and all things to do with the sea and, above all, there was and is, agriculture.

Coal was mined in the forest of Coedrath, near Saundersfoot, in the fourteenth century and by 1700 it was the chief export industry. It was shipped to St Helena for use in a jute factory, and to Singapore for tin smelting. Nearer home, it fired the blacksmith's forge, malt kilns and limekilns. Above all, it kept domestic fires burning, for which purpose the coal dust or culm was mixed with pounded clay, and the messy aggregate was placed on the fire, either with a shovel or by hand, after having been moulded into egg-shaped 'balls'. The culm fires were kept alight day and night, year after year.

The coal measures stretch in a belt from Carmarthen Bay to St

Bride's Bay, as an extension of the South Wales Coalfield. Owing to earth movements that occurred after the carboniferous rocks had been laid down, the seams are irregular and heavily faulted and therefore difficult to work. At first, the sloping seams were exploited, then shallow pits were dug, and then deeper ones. The coal was raised by windlass, worked by women. When a steam engine was introduced, in 1800, it became possible to reach the deeper veins and, by 1815, a third of the anthracite coal mined in South Wales, amounting to 185,000 tonnes, came from the Pembrokeshire Coalfield.

The coalfield was divided into three sections: Saundersfoot, Daugleddau and St Bride's Bay. The Saundersfoot section included the Bonville's Court Colliery which employed 300 men until it closed in 1930, and the Kilgetty and Broom Collieries which were worked up to the outbreak of the last war, when mining ceased in the area. Until 1830, when railway lines were laid to the newly-built harbour at Saundersfoot, the coal was taken by horse and cart, or by bullock waggon, from the collieries to Saundersfoot, Coppet Hall or Wiseman's Bridge and there loaded at low tide on to beached sailing vessels. Saundersfoot exported over thirty thousand tonnes annually.

Five collieries to the east of the Daugleddau produced more than ten thousand tonnes of coal and culm each year, most of which was exported from Landshipping. In 1844 the tide broke into the Garden Pit, near Landshipping Quay, and more than forty miners, including some young boys, were drowned. Coal from collieries around Jeffreston was exported from Cresswell Quay. On the western side, the Hook colliery produced forty-three-thousand tonnes at its peak in 1934 and continued in production until 1948. The coal was shipped from several small quays, of which there are remains at Little Milford and Lower Hook. When larger sea-going vessels were built in the middle of the last century, the coal was taken by barge to Lawrenny and Llangwm for further export, but a railway was built in 1929 connecting Hook with the main line at Johnston.

The coal measures extend westward to the coast and continue under the sea bed in St Bride's Bay. The Newgale and Nolton coalfield contained six collieries, including the Trefran Cliff Colliery, the red-brick chimney-stack of which still stands below the coast road, although the colliery closed in 1905. Vessels were loaded on the beach at Little Haven, or at the quay at Nolton Haven.

The difficulty in working shattered seams, the failure to introduce modern techniques and to invest in new workings, and the competition of larger and more conveniently placed coalfields, combined to bring

Little Haven, formerly a coal exporting port, is now a popular holiday resort
(*Wales Tourist Board*)

the exploitation of the Pembrokeshire Coalfield to an end soon after
the end of World War II.

Traces of iron-ore mines are visible in the cliffs near Coppet Hall,
along the track of the railway that ran between Saundersfoot harbour
and the Stepaside Iron Works, established by the Pembrokeshire Iron
and Coal Company in 1849. In 1864 some three-thousand tonnes of
pig iron, and a large quantity of iron ore, were exported from
Saundersfoot, but production ceased in 1877. The ruined walls of the
casting shed and of the workshops at Stepaside remain, together with
remnants of two blast furnaces, and traces of a canal, railway lines and a
causeway built by Thomas Telford.

Copper was mined in the cliffs overlooking Ramsey Sound on the St
David's Peninsula, at St Elvis and near Dale. Manganese ore was found
near Fishguard and at Ambleston. A silver-lead mine was worked at
Llanfyrnach, from 1764 to 1891 and produced seventeen-hundred
tonnes during its peak year, 1881, when the price of lead was £13 per

ton. The discovery of gold 'caused great rejoicing at Kilgerran and neighbouring villages' according to one report, but no more was heard of the find.

Stone from the St Bride's Quarries at Porthgain was used in the erection of public buildings in Liverpool, London and Dublin, and crushed to surface the streets of Bristol and the roads of Kent. The Porthgain Village Industries Limited, established in 1878, also operated a thriving brick works and built a harbour out of which over a hundred vessels carried around forty-thousand tonnes of granite each year.

Slate was used for roofing, flooring, walls and buildings, particularly in north Pembrokeshire where it was readily available. Slate from the local quarry was used in the rebuilding of Cilgerran Castle in 1225 and there are records of slate from the Gilfach quarry being used in domestic buildings around the same time. A cargo of 11,000 slates, quarried from the cliffs, was exported from Newport in 1566, and the export of slate from Abereiddi continued into the present century. The main quarries in the Presely Hills were at Rosebush, Tyrch and Glogue, and production continued until the outbreak of war. The slates varied in colour from blue-black to silver-grey, browns and greens. The silver-grey slates that roof the Palace of Westminster came from Llangolman, and slates from the locality have been used as far afield as Cape Town.

The acid soils of Pembrokeshire were improved by lime. Limestone quarried in south Pembrokeshire was shipped in small coastal vessels to feed the 150 limekilns that stood in almost every bay and inlet around the coast and on the off-shore islands. Another 120 kilns, built along the carboniferous limestone exposures, had a plentiful supply close at hand. The limestone was burned over a culm fire in a limekiln and, after cooling, was extracted through the 'kiln's eyes' – apertures at the bottom of the kiln. It was carried on to the land and laid in heaps to await a shower of rain, which would reduce it to a powder, ready to be spread. When lime came to be produced industrially and delivered to railheads, the limekiln fires went out, although they continued to burn at Haverfordwest until 1936, and at Tenby even later. By today, limekilns are regarded as ancient monuments and those that have escaped destruction are being carefully preserved.

Shipbuilding was a leading industry in Pembrokeshire for many centuries. Small schooners and sloops, usually of less than forty tons, were built at Newport, Fishguard, Solva and other coastal settlements, and along Milford Haven from Angle and Dale to Haverfordwest, until the middle of the last century. Shipyards at Milford, Neyland and Pembroke Dock then began to build barques, brigantines and larger

Porth-gain harbour built for the export of bricks and crushed roadstone (*Wales Tourist Board*)

ships. By the end of the century, naval vessels were launched at Milford but in 1814 the Royal Naval Dockyard was moved to Pembroke Dock. From then, until the closure of the dockyard in 1926, over 250 ships were built there, including the first steam man-o'-war, the first warship to be driven by a screw propeller, and the *Victoria and Albert*, the first of several royal yachts.

Agriculture

Unlike the other national parks, the Pembrokeshire Coast National Park has much of its area under agriculture, for this forms the main industry of Pembrokeshire. There have been farmers there since the Neolithic people during the fourth millennium BC brought with them knowledge of the cultivation and domestication of animals. Stone walls built by men of the Early Iron Age to encompass fields and enclosures still stand on St David's Head and on Skomer Island, indicating a continuity of agriculture for the past 2,000 years.

The tale of 'Manawydan son of Llyr' in *The Mabinogion*, the earliest recorded Welsh tales, tells how Manawydan came to Narberth and brought with him 'a burden of wheat' which he sowed in three crofts nearby, but when the wheat was ready for reaping it was completely devoured by mice, all of which escaped save one. Manawydan was dissuaded from hanging the miscreant when he found that the mouse was the transformed wife of Llwyd son of Cil Coed who had cast a spell over the land of Dyfed in settlement of an old score. She was soon changed back into 'the fairest young woman that any one had seen'. In the tale of 'Math son of Mathonwy', the magician Gwydion states that he had heard that 'small animals, their flesh better than the flesh of oxen', had been sent to Pryderi, prince of Dyfed, by the king of Annwn, the Celtic Hades, and that they were known as *moch* (swine). Gwydion and his men came to the court of Pryderi in the guise of bards and, by magic, purloined the pigs and drove them to the fastnesses of Snowdonia.

In the twelfth century Giraldus Cambrensis describes his country-men as a pastoral people living on the product of their herds, eating more meat than corn, and caring little for agriculture. He complains that they would not pay their tithes of wool and cheese until he threatened them with excommunication.

George Owen regrets, four centuries later, that better use was not made of the land and, in advocating methods for its improvement, quotes a contemporary saying that 'a man doth sand for himself, lime for his son and marl for his grand child'. His description of clay marl, although he attributes its origins to Noah's Flood, is possibly the earliest mention of boulder clay or glacial till. He claims that it was first used in Wales in about 1400 by a member of the Cole family of Llwyn-gwair. He regarded it as 'a sovereign medicine ordained by the goodness of God to cure the barreness of divers kinds of ground' and not only did he expound upon the subject in his 'Treatise of Marle' but also devised a special implement, his 'marl slice', for digging in the marl pits.

From the eighteenth century onward landowners and farmers got together to form farmers' clubs and agricultural societies that encouraged the improvement of the land and the stock, and offered rewards for good husbandry. The Society for Agriculture of Pembrokeshire was established in 1784 and others followed. Even so, Charles Hassall in his report 'A General View of the Agriculture of the County of Pembroke', that appeared in 1794, commented that 'the inhabitants of this county are not forward in receiving improvements in agriculture' and noted that 'a general prejudice seems to pervade the people against anything

new or differing in any respect from the old and beaten track in which they and their forefathers have trod'.

There were progressive farmers, however, among whom was John Mirehouse of Brownslade who in 1800 received the Gold Medal of the Society for the Encouragement of Arts, Science and Commerce. He had reclaimed a large area of marshland by deep drainage and converted it into the most valuable land in Castlemartin.

Mirehouse and his neighbours, the Campbells, later Earls Cawdor, of Stackpole, were foremost breeders of the famous Castlemartin Black cattle. Oxen of the breed were used as draught beasts and were notorious for their reckless speed which, it was said, would win them any chariot race.

From the fifteenth century onwards Welsh cattle were driven in herds to the Midlands and to London, notably to Smithfield Market, along established routes, invariably avoiding the toll-ridden turnpike roads. The routes are sometimes remembered in England by such names as the Welsh Road in Warwickshire, the Welsh Way in Gloucestershire and the Welsh Ride in Hampshire. In Hampshire there was formerly a Drovers' Inn at Stockbridge bearing an inscription in Welsh on its front wall offering seasoned hay, sweet grass, good beer and a comfortable bed. The drovers provided a link with the English world of commerce and, as middlemen in the cattle trade, had to be entrusted with large amounts of money. One of their number, in 1799, founded a bank at Llandovery, later to become famous as the Black Ox Bank.

For many years the Friesian has been the dominant breed in Pembrokeshire. Its cows will give a milk yield of 3,000 gallons (13,600 litres) a year and its male calves, sired by a Hereford bull, fatten into good beef animals.

It is sometimes said that there are more sheep than people in Pembrokeshire: in fact, there are nearly twice as many. Most are of the Welsh Mountain breed inhabiting the common rough grazing on the Presely Hills, and each sheep bears the earmark of its owner, allocated to him by the Presely bailiff.

Giraldus Cambrensis observed that the Welsh were 'a people with wide experience of woollen manufacturing but who paid no attention to industry or commerce'. By the fourteenth century, however, there

Storage hoppers at Porthgain from which graded stone was loaded into vessels for export (*B. R. Munt*)

Stackpole Quay, carved out of a limestone quarry (*Wales Tourist Board*)

was a considerable export trade in wool and woollen goods, mainly to Bristol and from there to France, Portugal and even Iceland. In 1326, Haverfordwest was the only staple town in Wales but, thirty years later, it was superseded by Carmarthen which exported 130,000 fleeces each year. During the course of the fourteenth century, following the introduction of technical innovations, including the application of water power to the fulling process, the woollen manufacturing industry developed rapidly. The fulling mill, or *pandy*, had hammers for scouring and beating, or fulling, the cloth three times, after it had been treated with urine, fuller's earth and soap and before a final washing.

Pembrokeshire acquired its first *pandy* in about 1300 and soon it had more than any other county in Wales, but the industry was pursued mainly in cottages and scattered homesteads and was without organisation. The cloth produced in Pembrokeshire was, therefore, rough and, at the beginning of the fifteenth century, it was of such inferior quality that it was given to the poor on Ash Wednesday. By 1600, the industry had virtually ceased to exist in Pembrokeshire, due, it was said, to an epidemic of 'sweating sickness', but raw wool was exported to North Wales and to England. Domestic spinning and weaving continued, and small factories began to appear from about 1650 onward.

With the invention of carding and spinning machinery in the early nineteenth century, there was a sharp increase in the number of woollen factories. To these, farmers brought their wool to be spun and woven for their own uses, and the surplus cloth was sold at local markets.

The factories were established along swift-flowing streams so as to make use of water power to drive the mules and carding engines, and were often situated in remote and isolated valleys. There were over thirty such factories still in operation in Pembrokeshire at the beginning of the present century but, by today, there remain only three: Tregwynt Factory, near St Nicholas, which was probably established as a *pandy* in the fourteenth century, Wallis Woollen Mill, near Ambleston, and Middle Mill, near Solva. They produce a wide range of textiles, including tweeds, tapestries, blankets, honeycomb bed covers, rugs and knitting wools.

5
LEISURE AND ART
IN PEMBROKESHIRE

Sport and Recreation

'Of pastimes and recreations fitte for gentlemen', wrote George Owen in about 1600, 'this county is not destitute in such solaces'. He states that the chief pastimes were hunting, hawking and fishing, and the recreations included wrestling, throwing the stone, bar and sledge-hammer, and archery. Bowls and tennis were also played, although they were prohibited under an Act of 1542 for the 'maytenance of artyllerie and debarringe of unlawful games'.

'A game of great antiquity', in which Owen had taken part and bore the marks on his head, hands and other parts of his body, was knappan. This was played with a hardwood ball well boiled in tallow, and resembled a Cornish game called 'hurling in the country'. It was traditionally played on feast days between adjoining parishes, with several hundreds of men, both mounted and on foot. The players wore only a light pair of breeches, as any other garment would be torn to pieces in the fury of the game. Those on horseback carried cudgels which they used freely on an opponent who refused to yield the ball, and players would return home 'with broken heads, black faces, bruised bodies and lame legs, yet laughing and merrily jesting'. The game was played on Newport Sands on Shrove Tuesday between men of the parishes of Newport and Nevern, but the great occasions were on Ascension Day and Corpus

Christi when the men of Cemais played the men of the lordship of Emlyn, with the men of Cardiganshire with them, in the presence of thousands of onlookers who took advantage of the occasion to eat, drink and be merry.

In other parts of Pembrokeshire, on Shrove Tuesday, a free-for-all game was played with a ball made of a bull's bladder covered in leather, during which game the players fortified themselves with pancakes, from baskets carried by the women. At Tenby the players numbered up to 300. At Narberth the game continued until 1890, but elsewhere it was stopped by magistrates on account of fighting and drunkenness.

Cards, dice and chess were all played in medieval times. In the parish of Whitechurch, to the north of the Presely Hills, chess was played by 'even the meanest ploughman' and the inhabitants had Welsh names for the chess pieces. The castles, or rooks, were known as *brain Owen ab Urien*, after Owen the son of Urien, the Welsh king of Rheged, on the Solway Firth, who bore a raven on his banner. A tale in *The Mabinogion* relates how Owen's 'host of ravens' attacked the knights of King Arthur while Owen and Arthur played chess with pieces of gold on a silver chessboard.

With a coastline of almost 180 miles (300km), it is only to be expected that the main recreational attractions of Pembrokeshire today are to do with the sea, but there are also facilities for those who prefer to enjoy their leisure on land.

There are scores of beaches, some with stretches of golden sand, some in secluded coves, where one may enjoy a bathe in the sea. Most of them are safe, but care should always be taken and warning notices on dangerous beaches should be heeded at all times. There are swimming-pools at Haverfordwest, Milford, Pembroke Dock and Tenby.

There are yacht clubs, or sailing centres, at a number of places around the coast and in Milford Haven, including Newport, Fishguard, Solva, Dale, Gelliswick, Lawrenny, Tenby and Saundersfoot. Beaches such as Cwmyreglwys and Little Haven are popular with dinghy sailors and several beaches are suitable for wind-surfing.

The coastal waters provide excellent fishing, either by beach-casting or by off-shore fishing from a boat. Newgale is rated as one of the six best beaches in Wales for white-water surf-fishing, and from the rocks in a number of places anglers may fish for mackerel, pollack, bass and conger eel. Off-shore fishing may yield cod, whiting, pollack, mackerel, skate, ray, wrasse, bass and dogfish, and off Saundersfoot there is shark and tope fishing. A tope caught there in 1964 weighed 74lb (33.5kg)

Solva harbour, a favourite yachting centre (*Wales Tourist Board*)

and created a world record. Bosherston Pools are good for coarse
fishing, with roach, perch, tench, and pike up to 30 lb (14kg). The
main game-fishing rivers are the Eastern and Western Cleddau, the
Teifi, the Nevern and the Gwaun, with salmon found in the larger
rivers, and migratory trout, locally known as sewin. The reservoirs at
Llys-y-frân and Rosebush are stocked with brown and rainbow trout.

Riding and pony-trekking are popular pastimes for which there is
provision at a number of establishments, several of which provide
tuition. Others offer accommodation packages as well.

There are 18-hole golf courses at Haverfordwest, Milford and Tenby,
and 9-hole courses at Newport, St David's and Pembroke Dock, and
there are bowling greens at Fishguard, Haverfordwest, Milford, Pembroke Dock, Tenby and Saundersfoot, and indoor bowling at Milford.
Tennis courts are available at Newport, Dinas, Wolfscastle, Haverfordwest, Milford, Pembroke Dock, Tenby and Saundersfoot; squash
courts at Wolfscastle, Haverfordwest, Neyland and Pembroke Dock;

badminton, basket-ball and volley-ball may be played at the Haver-fordwest Sports Centre.

Other activities that may be pursued during holidays include land-yachting, go-karting, parascending, gliding, rock-climbing, abseiling, canoeing, orienteering and field archery.

Art and Artists

Despite its varied landscapes and wealth of subject matter, Pembroke-shire has not produced many artists, and those that have achieved any fame are few in number.

Thomas George, the miniature artist, was born in Fishguard around 1790. He moved to London and exhibited at the Royal Academy on five occasions between 1829 and 1838. Among his few surviving works are a miniature on iron at the Victoria and Albert Museum, and a miniature and three watercolours at the National Museum of Wales. He moved to Madeira for reasons of health and died there in 1840.

Benjamin Phelps Gibbon, a native of Penally, became a line-engraver. He engraved several works after Edwin Landseer and among his engraved portraits is one of Queen Victoria after William Fowler.

James Milo Griffith, born in 1843 at Pontsely near Abercuch, was a sculptor. The Royal Academy accepted eight of his works in one year, the maximum number admissible, and among his sculptures are 'The Fine Arts' on Holborn Viaduct, 'The Four Evangelists' in Bristol Cathedral, and the statue of Sir Hugh Owen at Caernarvon.

Augustus John was born in 1878 in Tenby. His mother had gone there for safety as there had been a recent epidemic of scarlet fever at Haverfordwest where the family lived. It was at Haverfordwest during his early childhood and while staying with relatives at Begelly in a house overlooking Kingsmoor Common, with its gypsy encampment, that he first felt his great kinship with gypsies. 'The example of the nomads in their caravans below' he later wrote 'conspired to stir up dis-content and longing for a wider, freer world'.

His sister, Gwen John, born at Haverfordwest in 1876, is now re-garded as a greater artist than her brother. From 1898 onward she lived mostly in France, for a time friendly with Rodin and often in dire poverty. At the outbreak of war she tried to escape but died at Dieppe in 1939.

The nave of St David's Cathedral showing the sloping floor, leaning arcades, reredos and carved oak roof (*Roger Worsley*)

Maurice Sheppard, a native of Haverfordwest, has received national recognition as an artist and as President of the Royal Society of Painters in Watercolours.

Among those who found inspiration in Pembrokeshire were Richard Wilson, J. M. W. Turner and Peter de Wint who all painted Cilgerran Castle. Paul Sandby produced a haunting picture of Pembroke Castle, and William Frith placed Tenby Castle in the distant background of his delightful portrait of 'The Prawnseller of Tenby', the partner to which, 'The Tenby Fisherwoman', now hangs at the Castle Museum in Haverfordwest.

Charles Norris, who was born at Hughenden Manor near Beaconsfield, came to live at Milford Haven in 1800, where he remained for ten years before moving to Tenby. He worked in Pembrokeshire until his death in 1858 and produced a great mass of topographical works, most of which are drawings and etchings portraying local scenes, notably of St David's, Pembroke and Tenby. Some of these are displayed at the Tenby Museum.

Henry Gastineau had twenty-eight of his drawings of the Pembrokeshire scene included in *Wales, Illustrated in a Series of Views engraved on Steel from Original Drawings by Henry Gastineau,* published in 1830. Sir Richard Colt Hoare provided illustrations for *Historical Tour through Pembrokeshire* which in 1810 he had persuaded his friend Richard Fenton to publish.

Michael Ayrton, David Jones, Ceri Richards and John Piper came and were inspired there and, above all others, Graham Sutherland. Sutherland made his first visit to Pembrokeshire in 1934 and, in his own words, 'came upon two very remarkable passages of country situated in the arms of land which embrace the great area of St Bride's Bay'. The northern arm, the St David's Peninsula, intrigued him, with its tightly packed strips of fields, its majestic monadnocks, steep valleys and arabesque of roads. Travelling along the southern arm, he descended a green lane, buried in trees, which led to Sandy Haven, where herons gathered and the quality of light was 'magical and transforming'. For the next fifty years he was a regular visitor to Pembrokeshire, where he found:

the twisted gorse on the cliff edge, such as suggested the picture 'Gorse on Sea Wall' – twigs, like snakes, lying on the path, the bare rock, worn,

Porth Clais, where King Arthur is said to have landed in pursuit of the legendary wild boar *Twrch Trwyth (Roger Worsley)*

and showing through the path, heath fires, gorse burnt and blackened after fire, a tin school in an exuberant landscape, the high over-hanging hedges by the steep roads which pinch the setting sun, mantling clouds against a black sky and the thunder, the flowers and damp hollows, the farmer galloping on his horse down the estuary, the deep green valleys and the rounded hills and the whole structure, simple and complex. It was in this country that I began to learn painting.

The Graham Sutherland Gallery at Picton Castle has the largest collection of his works and is open to the public during the summer months. It was established in 1976 as a gift by the artist to the people of Pembrokeshire.

Tenby Museum has an art gallery in which there is a selection of drawings by Charles Norris and portraits by Augustus and Gwen John.

The Castle Museum and the County Library at Haverfordwest, and St Mary's Hall at St David's, have exhibitions of works by various artists.

Since the last war, Pembrokeshire has become increasingly the haunt of artists and, by today, there are artist-run galleries in most of the towns and in many of the villages.

6
WILD LIFE AND NATURE CONSERVATION

Plants

There are over a thousand recorded species of plants in Pembrokeshire, growing in a wide variety of natural and semi-natural habitats. The first list was published in the *Phytologist* in 1853 by Edwin Lees, and this was followed ten years later in the *Journal of Botany* with a list of 550 species, observed in the Tenby and Stackpole areas by C. C. Babington, Professor of Botany at Cambridge. Several other lists were published, all for the Tenby and St David's districts, and it was not until 1950 that the whole county was covered, in the *List of Pembrokeshire Plants* by Mrs F. L. Rees of Tenby. This contained 740 species of flowering plants. In 1970 the West Wales Naturalists' Trust published *Plants of Pembrokeshire* by T. A. Warren Davis FLS, County Recorder for the Botanical Society of the British Isles. In it are listed 1,016 of the 1,400 species recorded in Wales.

Spring has come to Pembrokeshire when the lesser celandine shows its shining yellow face at the foot of the wayside hedgerow. There soon follows the lesser stitchwort on its slender stem, the pale primrose, and the dog-violet that fades too soon. The verges become a ribbon of dandelion, and hedgebanks, even remote from the sea, have splashes of the scurvy-grass which once provided an antiscorbutic remedy for sailors and centurions. From the tops of the banks fall billowy clouds of blackthorn blossom.

With the arrival of summer the hedgerows in many places are an in-credible riot of colour: lady's smock and germander speedwell; cow parsley, in long curtains of white lace; the blue buttons of sheepsbit scabious; red campion and clover; dog-rose and bramble; tall foxgloves and spikes of pennywort; the milky foam of meadowsweet; alexanders, with yellow umbels and glossy leaves of green chartreuse; and birdsfoot trefoil, that has seventy other names. Lanes hang with the fragrance of honeysuckle and gorse, and are lined with field scabious and knapweed, toadflax and tufted vetch, lady's bedstraw, agrimony, St John's wort, centaury, harebell – the pale blue fairy's thimble, and biting stonecrop that some charitable wife named 'Welcome-home-husband-though-never-so-drunk'.

The hills in late summer are clad in a mantle of purple and gold heather and gorse. Bog asphodel is in abundance, and there is round-leaved sundew, bog St John's wort, ivy-leaved bell-flower and bilberry. Less common are bog myrtle, hare's tail cotton sedge, western butter-wort, cranberry and bog orchid. Stag's-horn and fir clubmoss occur sparingly on dry heath.

At various times woodland floors are carpeted in bluebells, ramsons, wood sorrel, wood anemone and occasionally wood spurge. The royal fern is not uncommon, and the southern polypody is found on lime-stone walls, and growing on trees in acid oak woodland at Burton. The Tunbridge filmy-fern occurs near Treffgarne, and Wilson's filmy-fern in the Presely Hills.

Pastures that were once floral fields full of clover, yellow rattle, eye-bright, cowslip and buttercups that have 'enough names to make up a Welshman's pedigree', are now a uniform green, and the wind blows waves across fields of barley that are no longer brightened by scarlet field poppy, cornflower, corn cockle and hatridge – as charlock is known here.

The fields around Tenby were covered at one time by Tenby daffodils (*Narcissus obvallaris*), so named by R. A. Salisbury in 1796. This daffodil has a uniformly deep-yellow flower, with the trumpet longer than the perianth leaves. Its origin is a mystery: it is most closely related to *Narcissus hispanicus,* a native of the Pyrenees and south-west France. Its uniqueness, however, was its downfall. During the nineteenth cen-tury, the trade value of its bulbs came to be realised and, during the 1880s half a million were sent to London in two years. The ploughing of grassland further speeded its extermination in Tenby's fields. Clutches survive on the hedgebanks of old or deserted cottages over a wide area of West Wales.

The Tenby daffodil (*J. W. Donovan*)

Along the cliffs there are plants that occur in few other places. Between St Ann's Head and Cemais Head, the prostrate broom grows sporadically, clinging close to the ground or rock face, and hairy greenweed, like a lesser version of the broom, may be found on the St David's Peninsula and on Strumble Head. A rock sea lavender found growing near Giltar Point in 1923 was given the name *Limonium transwallianum,* and another discovered on St David's Head in 1905 and occurring elsewhere only at Malin Head in County Donegal, was named *Limonium paradoxum.* The perennial centaury (*Centaurium portense*), discovered near Newport in September 1918, occurs in Britain only there and in west Cornwall, and abroad on the north-west coasts of France, Spain and Portugal.

Cliff-tops are matted with thrift and sea campion, vernal squill and cinquefoil, the scarlet pimpernel and occasionally the blue. On ledges and in nooks on the cliffs grow rock samphire, common and Danish scurvy-grass, sea spleenwort, kidney vetch, sea beet and wild cabbage – which George Owen of Henllys called sea cole. Roseroot, the only arctic-alpine species found there, is possibly at the southern limit of its range in Britain.

On marshes, bogs and wet heaths there are marsh orchids, bogbean, common fleabane, cotton grass, petty whin, wavy St John's wort, slender cicendia, yellow bartsia, common and pale butterwort, marsh stitchwort and lesser bladderwort. Fibrous tussock-sedge appears in the acid fen of saturated peat on Dowrog Common.

Sand blown landward forms dunes that are bonded by marram grass, among which appear sea bindweed, sea pansy, burnet rose, sea radish, squinancywort, ploughman's spikenard, blue fleabane, sea rocket, restharrow and carline thistle. Bee orchids and autumn lady's tresses, once widely spread, are now uncommon. The dune gentian (*Gentianella uliginosa*), found 'in a damp sandy pasture around Tenby' in 1923, was the first recorded find in Britain.

Salt marshes in autumn are often covered with sea asters and sea purslane, and the lax-flowered sea lavender that flourishes along the Daugleddau takes the place of the common sea lavender which does not extend this far west. Cord-grass (*Spartina anglica*), probably introduced on the Carew River about 1940, has spread to the tidal flats of Milford Haven, the Western and Eastern Cleddau, the Gann estuary, Sandy Haven and Poppit Sands.

Among the shingle and sand grow sea-kale, golden samphire, yellow-horned poppy and, more rarely, sea holly, the roots of which were once candied to make eryngoes for those who had 'no delight or appetite for venery'.

Apart from a few lichens, the plants of the rocky shore are seaweeds, green, brown and red, attached to the rocks by their holdfasts and obtaining their food from sea water. The green algae are most abundant in pools of the upper shore or where streams flow over the beach. The brown algae form in zones on the rocks. The highest, near the high-water mark of spring tides and which dries out almost black in colour during neap tides, is the channel wrack. Below it is the flat wrack, and then come bladder wrack, egg wrack and saw wrack, at the same level as which grow thong weed and bootlace weed. At and below water level are the kelps and oarweed that grow up to 10ft (3m) in length, their massive fronds connected to a branched holdfast by a leathery stipe.

The red algae include coral weed, Irish moss, edible dulse and sea spinach (*Porphyra umbilicalis*). The *Porphyra* is the weed that is made into *bara lawr* or laverbread. It is gathered along the Pembrokeshire coast at all times of the year but is best from April onward when the new growth begins, and after a strong receding tide has swept the sand clear of the rock where it grows. Its thin, irregularly shaped fronds are purplish-red in colour and become black and brittle when dried. After gathering it was at one time stored in low, reed-thatched huts. It is dispatched to the Swansea area for processing. There it is washed repeatedly and then boiled in a little salted water for up to twelve hours, according to the age and tenderness of the fronds, until it has become a dark gelatinous mass, resembling cooked spinach. It is usually eaten at breakfast, fried with bacon or rolled in oatmeal, and was popular with coal miners and manual workers. It has rich vitamins and a high protein content, and was believed to be a safeguard against goitre. It was also a fashionable dish in Bath in the eighteenth century and is nowadays promoted as 'Welsh caviare'.

Animals

The Pembrokeshire coast holds a third of the world population of the Atlantic grey seal (*Halichoerus grypus*), which is the largest mammal in Britain. There are no common seals (*Phoca vitulina*), even though these are found across the Irish Sea along the coasts of Ireland. The grey seal was hunted for its skin and blubber, and was regarded as an enemy by fishermen, so that its numbers were low until it was protected by the Grey Seals Protection Act of 1932. It appears around the coast, hauled out on off-shore rocks at low water, or its head may be seen bobbing in the sea and sometimes up-river as far as Haverfordwest. The main breeding colonies are on Ramsey, where some 200 pups are born each year, and on Skomer Island, which produces about 50, while around 100 more are born under mainland cliffs. With few exceptions the young are born in Pembrokeshire between September and November, and mostly during the latter half of September. The cow seeks a beach under high cliffs, or the interior of a cave, above high-water mark, to give birth. The pup (so called, in preference to 'calf', by the people of the coast) weighs around 30lb (14kg) at birth and rapidly puts on weight, feeding on its mother's milk which is eight times richer in fat content than the milk of a Jersey cow. At the end of the three-week lactation period it will have increased its weight threefold. It is born with a coat of white fur and is disinclined to take to the water until it is abandoned by its mother, usually in the fourth week, by which time it will have moulted its natal fur and acquired a dappled coat of light and dark grey.

At this stage it leaves its nursery beach and is prone to wander. A survey carried out by R. M. Lockley and members of the West Wales Naturalists' Trust over a period of twelve years revealed that grey seal pups born in Pembrokeshire travel incredible distances in a remarkably short space of time. Pups marked with a numbered flipper tag were found within weeks on the coasts of western Ireland, Cornwall and Brittany, and one had reached Santander, on the north coast of Spain, ten weeks after it had been born on Ramsey.

The cow reaches oestrus while still rearing its young and the master bull, patrolling the nursery beach, begins to pursue her until coition takes place, normally in the sea. The fertilised ovum does not develop into a foetus, however, until the following spring when the cow has regained the weight lost during nursing, about 100lb (45kg), and completed her moult. Delayed implantation then takes place and the true pregnancy period of seven and a half months begins.

Seals normally feed over high tide and, as the tide ebbs, they haul out on to their favourite rocks and sleep peacefully until the next tide.

Porpoise and dolphins are frequently seen off-shore, and there are occasional appearances of killer whale, as well as records of pilot and minke whales. During recent years, solitary dolphins have appeared and behaved as though they were seeking the fellowship of human beings. A male bottle-nosed dolphin (*Tursiops truncatus*) settled at Martin's Haven during the mid-1970s and was seen daily playfully nudging a moored dinghy and its buoy, and accompanying the boat ferrying visitors to Skomer. It also swam with skin divers and was alleged to have shown a marked preference for the female of that species. In the summer of 1975 it was identified by Dr Horace Dobbs as Donald, the friendly dolphin that he had previously encountered at Port Erin in the Isle of Man three years earlier. It then moved to Cornwall, to Penlee and then to St Ives, where it continued to display unique friendliness to those with whom it came into contact. In the mid-1980s another dolphin spent much time in Solva harbour and obviously enjoyed the proximity of people.

The largest land mammals are the fox and the badger. Foxes have increased greatly in numbers since the abolition of the gin-trap, and badgers have held their numbers. Weasels and stoats are not as common as they were, but the polecat has spread from mid-Wales to the foothills of Presely and the Gwaun Valley. The otter has suffered severely from river clearance schemes and pollution, but mink, escaped from fur farms, have reached pest proportions.

Rabbits, introduced by the Normans, are recorded as a source of income from the fourteenth century until 1954, when they were practically exterminated by myxomatosis. The red squirrel, a not uncommon sight thirty years ago, has disappeared completely, but there are some hopes of its return. The introduced grey squirrel is fairly common.

Hedgehogs are everywhere, and molehills indicate a healthy mole population. The dormouse appears in one locality only, and little is known of the distribution of the harvest mouse. Common, pygmy and water shrews are common, and bank, field and water voles are to be found in their usual habitats. The Skomer vole is larger and more ruddy than the bank vole and appears to have no fear of man.

Among recorded species of bats are the greater and lesser horseshoe, long-eared, whiskered, natterer's bats, pipistrelle and barbastelle.

The slow-worm is the most abundant reptile. The adder is common on heaths, dunes and cliff slopes and the grass snake is found in woodland and damp places, but is less common. The common lizard is widespread, but does not appear on Skokholm. Frogs and toads are less numerous than they used to be, and the only newt recorded in Pembrokeshire is the palmate newt.

Fish

Almost a hundred species of fish have been identified off the coast within the 3 mile (5km) limit, including herring, mackerel, plaice, pollack, bass, wrasse, cod, mullet, whiting, conger, dogfish and tope. The harmless plankton-feeding basking shark is a summer visitor. River fish include brown trout, salmon and sewin, or sea trout, and reservoirs are stocked with brown and rainbow trout. Bosherston Pools have pike, tench, perch and roach.

Birds

Pembrokeshire has such a diversity of habitats that it possesses a greater selection of bird species than any other part of Wales. As it lies in the path of the spring and autumn migrations along the west coast of Britain, it has a preponderance of regular, and occasional, visitors, some of which are rarities that have not been recorded elsewhere in the principality.

The coast was remarkable for its birds as early as the ninth century when an unknown Welsh poet sang of the feasting and revelry, above 'the crying of birds', at the 'fine fortress that stands on the ninth wave' at Tenby, while 'hoarse seabirds haunt the crested crags' below.

Giraldus Cambrensis, in his twelfth-century *Itinerary through Wales* felt that he 'ought not to omit mentioning the falcons' of Pembrokeshire which 'exercised a most severe tyranny over the river and land birds' and proceeded to relate how Henry II, while making preparations for his voyage to Ireland in 1171, was minded to take to 'the diversion of hawking' and, seeing a peregrine falcon perched upon a rock, let loose the goshawk he carried on his left arm. The falcon, however, quickly soared to a great height and struck the goshawk, which fell dead at the feet of the king, who was so impressed with the performance that he 'sent every year, around the breeding season, for falcons bred in the sea cliffs of Pembrokeshire, as no better could be found in any part of his dominions'.

An interesting commentary on the birds of Pembrokeshire was provided at the end of the sixteenth century by George Owen of Henllys. His main concern was game fowl, the chief among which he rated 'the gull and the woodcocke'. The fledgeling gulls were 'followed with boates and taken swymminge' and were considered a very dainty dish. The woodcock were caught in cockroads, or rides, in the woods, where nets were set between trees, 'at cockshut time', which was twilight. In the hills were grouse and heathcock, and grey and golden plover, while breeding 'in the field' were partridge, quail, water rail, lapwing and lark. He also refers to the woodquist (wood pigeon), whyniard (shoveler), shovelard (spoonbill), puett (black-headed gull), the curlew knave (whimbrel), the gwilym (guillemot), the winter sock (fieldfare) and the pilwater (Manx shearwater). Herons bred in the cliffs, but chiefly in high trees to which they were allured by placing the skulls of horses on the branches. The puffin, though fowl in all respects, was reputed to be fish, but Owen confesses that, were he so ceremonious as to refrain from eating flesh at holy seasons he would 'hardly adventure to eate this fowle for fishe'.

Among 'the want and defects' of the county he lists the pheasant and the nightingale. There were no pheasants until Sir Thomas Perrot 'procured certain hens and cockes to be transported out of Ireland', which he placed in a grove adjoining his home at Haroldston House near Haverfordwest. The nightingale was not to be found in Pembrokeshire, not because the weather was too cold, or for the want of 'pleasant groves and valleys'. Nor does the author accept:

> the fable fathered upon Saint David who, as the tale goeth, being seriouse occupied in the night tyme in his divine orizons, was so troubled with the sweet tuninges of the nightingale as that he could not fasten his minde upon heavenlie cogitacions . . . praied unto th' almightie that from that tyme forward there might never a nightingale sing within his Dioces.

It never did sing, until the night of 12 May 1948 and throughout the remainder of that month in the valley below Pointz Castle, almost within earshot of the place where the patron saint was disturbed in his orisons.

The first attempt at compiling a list of Pembrokeshire birds appeared in the *Zoologist* in 1850 and 1851 under the heading 'A Catalogue of Birds taken in Pembrokeshire; with Observations on their Habits, Manners, etc, by Mr James Tracy'. Tracy was the son of one of Lord Cawdor's keepers at Stackpole and practised as a taxidermist in Pembroke. His expertise is indicated by the use as subjects for illustration in William Yarrell's *History of British Birds* of his stuffed birds, including a Greenland falcon and yellow-billed American cuckoo, both shot on the Stackpole estate. Tracy's 'Catalogue' was incomplete and he later provided information on omitted species. This information formed part of some notes supplied to the *Zoologist* in 1866 and 1869 by Thomas Dix, a native of Norfolk, who had been appointed agent to the Cilwendeg estate in north Pembrokeshire.

In 1894 there appeared *The Birds of Pembrokeshire and its Islands* by the Rev Murray A. Mathew MA FLS of Stone Hall, at one time vicar of Buckland Dinham in Somerset and co-author of *Birds of Devon*. In the former book he lists 236 species of birds recorded in Pembrokeshire. He expresses the view that the total is small in comparison with the British total of 368 but considers this to be due to the lack of observers. His list includes 81 resident birds, 27 summer visitors, 43 winter visitors, 80 passing migrants in spring and autumn, 54 occasional visitors, 15 'waifs and strays', 1 former resident (the black guillemot) and 4 introduced species (Egyptian goose, mute swan, pheasant and red-legged partridge). The 'waifs and strays' were accidental visitors and included melodious warbler, bee-eater, scops owl, glossy ibis, Baillon's crake, ruddy sheldrake, red-crested pochard, roseate tern, great shearwater and fulmar.

Over fifty years later, in 1949, the West Wales Field Society published *The Birds of Pembrokeshire* compiled by R. M. Lockley in collaboration with Geoffrey C. S. Ingram and H. Morrey Salmon. The 255 species recorded comprise 88 resident birds, and 23 summer visitors, giving a total of 111 breeding birds, together with 40 regular visitors and passage migrants and 104 occasional visitors. Among the rarities listed are the white-spotted bluethroat, Ortolan and Lapland buntings, hoopoe, Bonelli's warbler, the yellow-billed cuckoo, American bittern, and the nightingale in Pointz Castle valley.

The *Pembrokeshire Bird Report* of 1984, compiled by J. W. Donovan and G. H. Rees, lists 318 species, among which are little shearwater, little egret, white stork, ruddy duck, osprey, hobby, black guillemot, barred and Pallas's warblers, red-breasted flycatcher, rose-coloured starling and scarlet rosefinch. American visitors included lesser yellow-legs and Baird's and buff-breasted sandpipers. The collared dove first bred in 1962, the reed warbler in 1974 and the pied flycatcher in 1978, but the woodlark and the corn and cirl buntings have ceased to breed in recent years.

The Pembrokeshire coast provides ideal habitats for a wide range of bird species and particularly for sea birds that return to breed each spring, some of them in vast numbers. Whilst there are about 3,000 pairs of guillemots, razorbills and kittiwakes to be seen around the Stack Rocks and Stackpole Head, and smaller auk colonies along the north coast, notably at Needle Rock, Fishguard, and on Dinas Head, nothing compares with the spectacular displays that may be witnessed on the off-shore islands.

Along mainland cliff tops and in adjacent rough pasture, meadow pipits, skylarks and wheatear are common, while stonechats and yellowhammers call from gorse-bush and bramble. The chough, of which about 50 pairs breed along the coast, uses its curved red bill to dig for grubs and worms in the close-cropped turf.

Below the cliffs and on estuaries, among the birds that feed between the tides are dunlin, redshank, curlew, oystercatcher, turnstone, mallard, teal and shelduck.

Rabbit burrows provide convenient nesting holes for close on 10,000 pairs of puffins and 150,000 pairs of Manx shearwaters on the islands of Skomer and Skokholm. The shearwater spends the day at sea, often flying to feed on sardines off the north coast of Spain while its mate broods in the burrow. The single young bird is left to find its own way to the winter feeding grounds on the Atlantic coasts of South America. The storm petrel, Mother Carey's Chicken, also leaves its nesting crevice before the break of day and returns at nightfall, so that it is seldom seen except at sea 'walking the water'.

Grassholm has the largest gannet colony in England and Wales with 28,000 nests tightly packed on one side of the island. St Margaret's Island has the largest cormorant colony in Wales, with over 300 breeding pairs.

The fulmar petrel, which spread southward and first bred in Wales forty years ago, now occupies more than 500 nesting sites on Skomer and Skokholm alone. The peregrine falcon, reduced to a single eyrie twenty years ago, has made a remarkable recovery and now has some 20 eyries, but this is little more than half the pre-war number.

Buzzard and kestrel are not uncommon, and the red kite is an occa-

Razorbill, symbol of the Pembrokeshire Coast National Park

sional visitor. The goshawk is often seen, while the merlin and the hen harrier are winter raptors.

In the broad-leaved woodlands, nuthatch and tree creeper occur, and green woodpecker and great spotted woodpecker, and occasionally the lesser spotted. The coniferous plantations on the Presely Hills have attracted siskin, redpoll and redstart, and even black grouse.

Butterflies

With some forty species of butterflies, the Pembrokeshire Coast National Park is better endowed than most areas in Wales. Some of these are rare, like the brimstone, while the Camberwell beauty is an occasional migrant from northern Europe, and the monarch has been recorded as a stray transatlantic immigrant.

The bright sky-blue of the male common blue catches the eye along the coast path in springtime, the female being brown with varying touches of blue; with them the small copper with its metallic hue can be seen. Summer brings the meadow brown, dark green fritillary and the grayling, and occasionally the small blue which feeds on the kidney vetch. The brown argus visits the calcareous soils of south Pembrokeshire and may be seen along the limestone cliffs on sunny days.

The edges of woodlands and woodland clearings and glades are favourite habitats of a wide variety of butterflies, including speckled wood, comma, holly blue, most of the fritillaries, the green hairstreak and sometimes the brown hairstreak and, very rarely, the large tortoiseshell. The purple hairstreak seeks its larval foodplant high in the canopy of oakwoods, but the white-letter hairstreak has suffered on account of the ravages of the Dutch elm disease.

The green-veined white feeds in fields of charlock and other wild cruciferae while the large and small whites attack the garden varieties of brassica. The gardener is more than compensated for his loss of cabbage, especially if he has a buddleia, by the presence of the peacock and the painted lady, the small tortoiseshell and the resplendent red admiral.

On open ground and hedgebanks may be seen the hedge brown or gatekeeper, the wall brown and the meadow brown, ringlet, clouded yellow sometimes accompanied by the rarer pale clouded yellow, the orange tip where there is garlic mustard, and skippers, grizzled, dingy, and the large, the small and, very rarely, the Essex skippers.

The marsh fritillary feeds on devil's-bit scabious on bogland, and the small heath is the only regular to inhabit the hills.

These are but indications, for butterflies, though they favour certain habitats, may stray to another. Wherever they are to be seen, they should not be disturbed, nor their habitats in any way damaged.

Sea-shore Life

Between the tides, acorn barnacles and their chief predator – the common dog whelk, limpets and mussels cling to the bare rock, while periwinkles hold a firm grip beneath the seaweed cover. Starfish, sea urchins, prawns and crabs, sea anemones and tube worms inhabit the rocky pools. Shingle beaches harbour no form of life owing to their unstable nature, and on sandy shores animal life exists below the surface. The cockle and striped venus burrow superficially, but the razor shells are capable of disappearing vertically with great speed, and the tellins, with their flattened shells, are able to move rapidly through the sand. Lugworms betray their presence by leaving casts and hollows on the surface. The burrowing starfish, the sea potato, sand eels and the masked crab also live below the surface, low on the shore. In sand, or sandy mud, the sand gaper, the edible American 'soft-shelled clam', and the peppery furrow shell, are common.

The wealth and variety of shore life attracted the attention of George Eliot while on a visit to Tenby in 1856, and her companion George Henry Lewes 'ransacked the sea' for specimens, while Philip Henry Gosse, at the same time, marvelled in his *Tenby, a Seaside Holiday* at 'the rare zoophytes, seaweeds, and anemones, which could be obtained at other points of the coasts of Britain only by dredging'.

Nature Conservation

Despite the interest shown by eminent naturalists in the plant and animal life of Pembrokeshire from the middle of the last century onward, and although the Royal Society for the Protection of Birds was established in 1889, and the Society for the Promotion of Nature Reserves in 1912, no serious attempt at nature conservation was made until 1933 when R. M. Lockley set up a bird observatory. This was on Skokholm, where he lived at that time and was the first in Britain. In 1938 he and Lionel Whitehead, who owned Ramsey, established the Pembrokeshire Bird Protection Society to take over the responsibilities of the RSPB in Pembrokeshire. The Society was invited to supervise the gannetry on Grassholm and to maintain the Skokholm Bird Observatory. Ramsey was declared a bird sanctuary and the owner of Skomer Island received a payment in return for prohibiting gin-traps, that were injurious to birds. In 1944 the Society secured a lease of Cardigan Island, which it later purchased.

The Society extended its area of influence in 1945 to cover in addition the counties of Carmarthen, Cardigan and Merioneth, and changed its name to the West Wales Field Society. In 1961 it was reconstituted as the West Wales Naturalists' Trust and, in 1984, it became known as the West Wales Trust for Nature Conservation.

The Trust owns, leases or manages over fifty nature reserves in West Wales including Skomer Island, which is a national nature reserve, Skokholm and St Margaret's Island, and the following, which are within, or near, the National Park.

Brunt Hill (SM 817073)
On the east bank of the Gann estuary, covered with bracken until Corsican and Lodgepole pines were planted from 1959 onward. Rhyolitic rocks of the Skomer volcanic series are exposed in outcrops along the northern half of the site, and in a disused quarry, in which oaks and birches have been planted.

Cardigan Island (SN 160516)
This 'forty acres or thereabouts of land surrounded by water', as the purchase deed described it, was held under lease from 1944 until it was bought in 1963. When the SS *Herefordshire* was wrecked on its northern point in 1934, brown rats from the ship came ashore and the island's colony of puffins dwindled away. The rats were exterminated by the Trust and efforts have been made to recolonise the puffins. Breeding birds include cormorant, shag, fulmar and gulls, and among visitors are chough, kittiwake, curlew and snow bunting. Grey seals are resident along the shore, and the Trust maintains a flock of Soay sheep on the island.

Cemais Head (SN 132502)
The fiftieth nature reserve acquired by the West Wales Trust for Nature Conservation, it is a bold promontory forming the southern arm of the Teifi estuary. It is composed of sedimentary rocks of the Ordovician period, folded and faulted during the Caledonian orogeny; the folds are well displayed on the westward side. Cormorants have a breeding colony in the cliffs, and choughs feed on the close-cropped sward. Fulmars, ravens and kestrels may be seen, and the occasional peregrine falcon. Grey seals frequently appear off shore, and small schools of porpoises and dolphins sometimes pass by. Across the estuary lies Cardigan Island and there is a panoramic view of Bardsey, the Lleyn Peninsula and Snowdonia on a clear day. The Trust has prepared a nature trail which skirts this reserve and in part follows the coast path.

As well as that on Cemais Head there are other nature trails within the National Park, as follows.

Dinas Island Nature Trail A promontory, though once insulated by a meltwater channel that now forms the steep-sided valley of Cwm Dewi, which passes through dark marine sandstone of the Ordovician period. Like Cemais Head, the headland has been dated as Silurian but is now regarded as late Ordovician. The nature trail follows the coast path for

Pentre Ifan, one of the finest burial chambers in the country (*Roger Worsley*)

Lower Fishguard, which was disguised as Llaregyb for the filming of *Under Milk Wood* (Roger Worsley)

much of the way, and it may be joined either at Cwmyreglwys (SN 016401) or at Pwllgwaelod (SN 005399).

Lydstep Head (SS 087978)
A promontory with precipitous cliffs, in the carboniferous limestone area of south Pembrokeshire, from which there is a splendid view of Caldey, St Margaret's Island and Proud Giltar. Among breeding birds are razorbill, guillemot and fulmar, while chough, puffin and peregrine may be seen. Rock samphire and other halophytic (salt tolerant) plants are found, along with thrift, rock sea lavender, sea beet, vernal squill, early purple orchid, common spotted orchid and green-winged orchid. The nature trail starts and finishes at a point near Lydstep Head car park, which may be reached from Lydstep Haven on payment of an entrance fee. It may also be reached on foot from Lydstep village (SS 086983). The trail is 1½ miles (2½km) long.

Marloes Nature Trail
Commences near the National Trust car park at SN 780082 and proceeds along Sandy Lane between high banks of blackthorn and bramble until it reaches the shore at Mill Beach, on Marloes Sands. The Silurian rocks in the cliffs were upended during the Armorican earth movements to such an extent that the Three Chimneys stand vertically. Gateholm is old red sandstone. The trail returns past the Marloes Mere nature reserve and the Runwayskiln Youth Hostel to the car park.

Coed Llwyngorres (SN 100390)
On the northern side of the Nevern Valley and extending from Velindre to the vicinity of Nevern, a mixed woodland, with oak dominant at its eastern end.

Dowrog Common (SM 769268)
With its freshwater pools and lowland moors this is an important habitat of threatened species. Its breeding birds include sedge warbler, coot, water rail, shoveler, curlew and short-eared owl, and there is a wide diversity of plant communities, including fibrous tussock-sedge (*Carex appropinquata*). Dragonflies are abundant and include the small red damsel-fly (*Ceriagrion tenellum*), and among the butterflies are the green hairstreak (*Callophrys rubi*) and the marsh fritillary (*Euphydryas aurinia*).

Felin-y-gigfran (SN 117373)
A steep slope in the Nevern valley with rugged outcrops of intrusive

Ordovician rocks giving it a spectacular beauty. The reserve provides a habitat for the dipper, heron and kingfisher.

Garn Turne (SM 979273)

An archaeological site containing a collapsed *cromlech* or burial chamber. The uprights lie beneath the massive capstone and there are traces of a funnel-shaped forecourt indicating that it may have been raised by the people who built Pentre Ifan after they had moved down from the northern shores of the Irish Sea about 2500BC.

Goodwick Moor (SM 946377)

A habitat of bog myrtle (*Myrica gale*) and of rare birds, including bittern, Baillon's crake, spotted crake, water rail, grey phalarope, spoonbill and green sandpiper.

Llannerch Alder Carr (SN 057353)

In the Gwaun Valley, a mature carr of alder (*Alnus glutinosa*) and sallow (*Salix cinerea* ssp. *oleifolia*) which, with its glades, tussocks and fallen trees, provides a variety of habitats.

Marloes Mere (SM 777082)

Reputed for its medicinal leeches during the nineteenth century. The leeches were obtained by stirring the waters and netting them as they came to the surface, and then they were dispatched to Harley Street. The water level was controlled by a sluice, to attract wildfowl for sporting purposes. The sluice, however, perished and a new one has been installed by the Trust. Curlew and reed bunting breed here, and migrants include green sandpiper, whimbrel and yellow wagtail.

Old Mill Grounds (SM 953161)

The site of a water-driven saw mill and a wooded slope on a bank of the Western Cleddau at Haverfordwest. The rare wood clubrush (*Scirpus sylvaticus*) is native here. Among the bird species are nuthatch, treecreeper, goldcrest, blackcap and grasshopper warbler.

Pembroke Upper Mill Pond (SM 993016)

Part of the tidal estuary of the Pembroke River until the mill bridge was built in the thirteenth century to store water to drive a tidal mill. The vegetation of the pond presents a transition from estuarine to freshwater conditions, and includes horned pondweed (*Zannichellia palustris*), rare in Pembrokeshire. Breeding birds include tufted duck, pochard, little grebe and kingfisher.

Pengelli Forest (SN 130392)

Where George Owen of Henllys bred sparrowhawks and had thirteen cockshoots, or open glades, for catching woodcock. It is the largest area of ancient woodland in Pembrokeshire, covering about 173 acres (70ha), and is designated a Site of Special Scientific Interest.

Portfield Gate Quarry (SM 923155)

Lies off the B4341 road from Haverfordwest to Broad Haven. When the quarry closed, the workings became flooded, forming two small pools.

Rosemoor (SM 874112)

Lies in a valley near Walwyn's Castle. The steep, east-facing slopes are composed of Silurian shales, while the valley bottom is of post-glacial alluvial deposits. Among breeding birds are great spotted woodpecker, spotted flycatcher, whitethroat, blackcap and bullfinch. Coot, moorhen, mallard and Canada goose nest at the man-made lake, which holds brown trout, eel, stoneloach and sticklebacks, and is visited by otters.

Sam's Wood (SN 004093)

A piece of ancient woodland that is typical of the oakwoods that clothe the steep slopes of the Daugleddau reaches. Notable tree species are spindle (*Euonymus europaeus*) and wild service (*Sorbus torminalis*).

Western Cleddau Mire (SM 896317)

Forms part of the largest remaining flood-plain mire in Wales and comprises a wide range of wetland habitats.

West Hook Cliffs (SM 762092)

Stretching along the southern shore of St Bride's Bay, of Silurian shales with volcanic intrusions of the Skomer series. The flora includes vernal squill (*Scilla verna*), heath spotted orchid (*Dactylorhiza maculata* ssp. *ericetorum*), the rare wood small-reed (*Calamagrostis epigeios*) and prostrate broom (*Sarothamnus scoparius* ssp. *maritimus*).

West Williamston (SN 027062)

A promontory at the confluence of the Carew and Cresswell rivers, deeply indented with tidal creeks excavated as loading bays during quarrying operations that were extensively carried on. Salt marsh and mud flats provide habitats for water and wading birds, and for plants, including marsh mallow. Over 50 species of lichen have been identified, and almost 30 species of fungi.

7
THE OFF-SHORE ISLANDS

The islands off the Pembrokeshire coast have been known to man since earliest times. Caves on Caldey gave shelter to those who came during the Old Stone Age, and Mesolithic men worked flints there, as they also did on Skokholm. Skomer was populated by Early Iron Age farmers, and Ramsey was a retreat of the Celtic saints. At Grassholm, legend says, the head of Brân the Blessed rested on its way to burial in London's White Mount.

Each island differs from the rest. Caldey is reserved for man's quiet contemplation, and compline as observed by the Cistercian Order of the Strict Obedience. Ramsey is the sanctuary of the grey seal. The others are for the birds. Yet each island, even in the raucous gossip of a myriad seabirds, has the peace of a sea-girt solitude remote from the cares of this world.

St Catherine's Rock
This is separated from the mainland by a fault in the carboniferous limestone. It takes its name from a chapel dedicated to St Catherine, the patron saint of spinners, upon the site of which, in 1869, was built a fort as part of the defences of Milford Haven.

Caldey
This is a detached part of the plateau of south Pembrokeshire. Its northern half is carboniferous limestone, its southern old red sandstone.

Nanna's Cave was occupied during the Palaeolithic Age and Daylight Rock was a flint-working site in the Middle Stone Age. Long before the Norsemen called it 'cold island', Caldey was Ynys Pŷr named after Pŷr who founded a monastery on the island and who, it is said, was drowned in a pond into which he fell 'while drunken with wine'. He was succeeded around 520AD by Samson, who later became bishop of Dol in Brittany. A relic of that period is the stone pillar standing in the nave of the old priory church and inscribed in ogham to the memory of Maglia Dubracunas, to which was added, in the ninth century, a Latin cross and the words: 'And by the sign of the Cross that I have fashioned I ask all who pass by to pray for the soul of Cadwgan'.

The early monastery was destroyed by the Norse and, in the twelfth century Robert Fitzmartin, lord of Cemais, gave Caldey to the monks of the Benedictine Abbey at St Dogmael's. After the Dissolution the island passed through many owners until it was purchased in 1897 by the Rev Dŏne Bushell, a Cardiff-born master at Harrow, who restored the church and other buildings. In 1906 it was sold to Father Aeldred who built the present Abbey, dedicated to St Samson, for the Reformed Order of Anglican Benedictines. Seven years later, Aeldred and most of the monks were converted to Rome, and in 1928, they left for

Caldey, with St Margaret's Island and the mainland in the background (*Countryside Commission*)

Prinknash Abbey. Caldey was sold to the Cistercians and was occupied by Trappist monks from Chimay, in Belgium, who farm the island.

The restored Church buildings are ranged round a cloister yard on the western side of which is the old gatehouse and a dovecote. The oldest part of the church is on the south side. The tower is surmounted by a stone spire that leans a yard out of the perpendicular. The refectory stood on the north side of the yard and on the east was the calefactory, the room in which the monks warmed themselves, with a dormitory over, reached by a stone staircase in the thickness of the wall. The kitchen was placed in the north-east corner and, above it, was the prior's chamber, with its garderobe. An inscribed stone stands on the south side of the nave.

The island was for centuries a haven for pirates. John Paul from Kirkudbright, who added Jones to his name when he joined the American Navy in 1775, dropped anchor in Paul Jones Bay and, for some inexplicable reason, his ghost walks the cliffs on moonlit nights.

Boats run regularly to the island during the summer, from Tenby harbour at high tide and from Castle Beach at low water, from Monday to Friday. A narrow, fuchsia-laden lane leads past a calvary and a watch tower, now converted into a chapel, the Chapel of Our Lady of Peace, on to the 'village' which has tea rooms, a gift shop, and a post office, where 'Caldey Island stamps' may be bought. For a number of years the monks have been selling perfumes and toiletries made from the gorse and other wild flowers on the island.

St Margaret's Island

This is joined to Caldey at low water. It once had a chapel, consecrated to St Margaret, but this and other buildings, possibly of monastic origin, became cottages for quarrymen. The limestone quarries were worked to such an extent that the island has shrunk to its present size. The island was heavily populated by puffins and Manx shearwaters until it was colonised by rats, but there are guillemot, razorbill, kittiwake and shag, and the finest breeding colony of cormorants in England and Wales. It is a nature reserve of the West Wales Trust for Nature Conservation.

Skokholm

The name was also spelt Stokholm in the thirteenth century, which may have been the original form. It is therefore difficult to know what was in the minds of the Norsemen when they gave it a name, but it is likely that they intended it to be known as 'the island in the sound'.

Like the Dale Peninsula, it is composed of old red sandstone, much folded, and was over-ridden by ice. It is 240 acres (100ha) in area, with little relief except for a few ridges and outcrops.

Surface flints provide evidence of a Mesolithic settlement, but there is no sign of Early Iron Age occupation. The earliest recorded history is of grants from 1230 onward by the Earls of Pembroke. In the eighteenth century it was acquired by the Allen family of Dale Castle, whose descendant still owns the island. It is leased to the West Wales Trust for Nature Conservation and is open to visitors. It was occupied, from 1927 to 1940 by the naturalist and author R. M. Lockley, who established the first Bird Observatory in Britain there in 1933. He restored the farmhouse and outbuildings using timbers from a wrecked schooner, the *Alice Williams*, the figurehead of which still stands above South Haven to greet the visitor.

The island bird list total 240 species, of which only 39 species breed, including around 35,000 pairs of Manx shearwater and over 6,000 pairs of storm petrel. The fulmar first bred in 1967 and there are now around 20 breeding sites. Recent rarities include little egret, stone curlew, Dartford warbler, little swift, rufous bush robin, snow goose and red-footed falcon. A few grey seals are seen offshore. Due to the absence of the flea vector of myxomatosis there is a high density of rabbits, which are smaller and darker than their mainland counterparts and varieties such as black, long-haired and white-collared occur with unusually high frequency. House mice, accidentally introduced in the 1890s are larger on average than mainland mice and rather darker in colour.

Over 270 species of flowering plants and ferns have been listed, and there are spectacular displays of bluebell, thrift, sea campion and vernal squill.

Gateholm (SM 769071)

This is a flat-topped mass of old red sandstone in the process of being separated from the mainland by marine erosion. Its surface is covered with the remains of a settlement of 130 small enclosures, or cells, mostly in rows, which could have accommodated around 250 persons. It was occupied during the early Christian period and may have been monastic, but there is no evidence of any ecclesiastical building.

Middleholm Island

Middleholm lies separated on the one hand from Skomer by Little Sound, and on the other from the mainland by Jack Sound. It covers 21 acres (8.5ha) and rises 170ft (52m) above sea level. A dry-stone wall running north and south partitions the island, on the east side of which are the remains of a small settlement comprising a two-roomed hut and an enclosure. As there is no fresh water on the island it is probable that this provided accommodation for ferreters or shepherds. Apart from rabbits, which are largely melanistic, there are no mammals. Breeding birds include Manx shearwater, cormorant, shag, guillemot, razorbill, puffin, oystercatcher, raven, carrion crow, skylark and meadow and rock pipits. Bracken covers the northern slopes and the vegetation otherwise is similar to that on Skomer.

Skomer Island

One of the finest seabird islands in the British Isles, Skomer is a national nature reserve managed by the West Wales Trust for Nature Conservation.

Up to 100,000 pairs of Manx shearwaters arrive each spring from the south Atlantic, to breed in the burrows that honeycomb the island. Other burrows are occupied by breeding puffins, of which there are now some 7,000 pairs compared with 50,000 a few decades ago. Guillemots lay single eggs exposed on narrow ledges on the cliff face, while razorbills secrete theirs in crevices or beneath boulders. The fulmar petrel, first recorded as a breeding species on the island in 1948, has over 200 cliff nesting sites. The 1,700 pairs of kittiwakes form the largest colony in Wales. Lesser black-backed gulls nest among the bluebells, 12,000 pairs of them, and 600 pairs of herring gulls nest along the cliff slopes. The greater black-headed gulls have had to be controlled on account of their predation on other species, notably the Manx shearwaters.

Breeding birds on the island also include the short-eared owl, buzzard, kestrel, chough, raven, cormorant, carrion crow, oystercatcher, lapwing, wheatear, skylark, stonechat and storm petrel. Among the rare species recorded on the island are the great skua, black tern, Alpine swift, hobby, melodious warbler, woodchat shrike, red-breasted flycatcher, serin and Lapland bunting.

Up to 150 Atlantic grey seals are present on some days and may be seen hauled out on outlying rocks at the Garland Stone and elsewhere, and about 50 pups are born on the beaches, or in caves, during September and October each year. The only land mammals are the rabbit, long-tailed field mouse, common and pygmy shrews, and the Skomer vole (Clethrionomys glareolus skomerensis), a unique bank vole.

In May Skomer is a carpet of bluebells, red campion, thrift and sea campion, while in June, battalions of foxgloves peer out of the bracken. Over 280 species of flowering plants and ferns have been recorded.

With its detached rocks, the island covers 722 acres (292ha). Its rocks are part of the Skomer Volcanic Group of the Lower Silurian period, formed around 420 million years ago. Its level tableland is an extension of the 200-foot (60m) mainland platform, and the presence of erratic boulders, one precariously balanced, shows that it was over-ridden by the Irish Sea glacier.

Evidence of human occupation during the Early Iron Age, probably in the first century BC, is provided by hut groups, enclosures and field systems. Dry-stone walls separate the fields and have large grounders at their base. The Norse called it Skalmey, from its cloven shape, but it has been known as Skomer since the eighteenth century. The Anglo-Normans used it as a highly profitable rabbit warren, and it was later grazed and exploited as a source of bird-meat and eggs. The farm build-ings, limekilns and quay were built in the 1840s. The farmhouse suf-fered irreparable damage in a storm in 1954, but the outbuildings provide accommodation for visitors.

A boat crosses from Martin's Haven. The island is open to visitors during the season, except Mondays, on payment of a landing fee. The sea around Skomer and the Marloes Peninsula is a marine nature reserve.

Grassholm

The Norsemen called this 'grass island', supplanting the old Welsh name Gwales where, according to a tale in *The Mabinogian*, there was 'a fair royal palace overlooking the sea'.

A century ago the island, of 22 acres (9ha), was populated by half a million puffins but they have deserted it for Skomer and Skokholm. At that time, there were 20 pairs of gannets nesting and it is now the largest gannetry in England and Wales with over 20,000 nests. Up to 100 grey seals haul out on the rocks around the island at low tide.

Grassholm continues the volcanic rocks of the Skomer series.

The Smalls

This is a cluster of rocks, a continuation of the volcanics of the Skomer series, beyond the half-tide reef of the Hats and Barrels. A lighthouse, prefabricated at Solva, was erected on The Smalls in 1775. During the winter of 1801 one of its two keepers died and his companion lashed the body, in a rough-made coffin, to the lantern rail, as he feared that he might be held responsible for the other man's death if he disposed of the body. After that incident, until recently when they have become fully automatic, lighthouses were always manned by no less than three keep-ers. The present lighthouse was built in 1861 of granite brought from quarries near Bodmin. This was taken to Solva, where it was trimmed, and it was shipped out of the specially built Trinity Quay. Nearby rocks are a favourite hauling-out site for grey seals.

Ramsey
It is believed to have been named after a Norseman, Hrafn. Ptolemy referred to it as Lymen and the Welsh name is given as Ynys Dyfanog. Dyfanog was a fellow saint of Justinian and they each had a chapel on the island, which is popularly known by the Welsh, however, as Ynys Dewi, 'David's Island'.

The island is 600 acres (240ha) in area and is a continuation of the mainland plateau of the St David's Peninsula, with rhyolitic hills rising at Carn Ysgubor, Carn Llundain and Foel Fawr. The sea has eroded narrow belts of shale leaving the small islands of Ynys Gwelltog, Ynys Cantwr and Ynys Beri and a number of stacks.

A legend states that the island was once connected to the mainland but Justinian, desiring solitude, prayed that it should be insulated, and nothing of the land bridge was left save The Bitches, jagged teeth of rocks through which fearsome tides flow. Ramsey Sound was, in fact, a valley submerged during the post-glacial period.

The island has been extensively farmed. In 1326 it was considered capable of holding a stock of 10 horses, 100 cattle and 300 sheep, and the Bishop of St David's, in whose lordship it lay, was entitled to take 500 rabbits. In recent years, a herd of deer was brought to graze.

Ramsey is the main sanctuary of the grey seal and around 200 pups are born on its beaches and in its caves each autumn.

Guillemots, razorbills and kittiwakes are the main breeding species, and chough, raven, buzzard, heron and peregrine falcon also breed.

The island has a varied flora including a number of rare plants, such as fiddle dock, subterranean clover, floating water plantain, royal fern and adder's-tongue fern. Juniper, the only conifer that appears to be truly native, grows on cliffs on the east side of the island.

Boats cross to the island from St Justinian's (SM 724252).

The Bishops and Clerks is the name given to a string of perilous rocks to the west of Ramsey which, according to George Owen, 'preach deadly doctrine to their winter audience'. The crew of a Swedish vessel, wrecked on these rocks in 1793, was rescued by Margaret Theodosia Williams of Treleddyn Farm, who was known as the 'Grace Darling of Pembrokeshire' thereafter. A lighthouse was erected on the South Bishop rock in 1840.

8
THE PRESELY HILLS

The Presely Hills stretch across north Pembrokeshire and although they do not reach great heights they achieve a dominance over the whole area. They form a range of rounded hills broken, here and there, by rocky crags, and their frequent appearance in Welsh legend and history indicates that they were held in special veneration from early times.

Apart from Foel Drygarn, the hills are composed of shales and mudstones of the Llanvirn beds laid down in the sea during the Ordovician period, with igneous rocks exposed in narrow strips. These extend in an east-north-east and west-south-west direction as a result of the massive folds of the Caledonian earth movement which have been eroded and worn down to their present form. The volcanic rocks are intrusive dolerite and diorite with bands of extrusive rhyolite along the southern slopes. The dolerites in the Carnmenyn area contain crystals of pink and white feldspar which enabled the area to be identified as the source of the bluestones of Stonehenge.

The whole area was over-ridden by the Irish Sea glacier, when ice covered the summits to a depth of 1,000ft (300m), and again, to a lesser degree, some 17,000 years ago. There are few traces of glaciation, however, apart from erratic boulders, some smoothing of rock surfaces, and some hollows deepened by nivation.

The plateaux of the broad summits may be the remnants of level surfaces produced when the sea level was 1,000ft (300m) higher than the present, and there is evidence of a wave-cut platform at 600ft (180m), particularly on the northern side. The lower slopes of the hills are covered in boulder clay which holds the 60in (150cm) of rain that falls annually, to produce extensive areas of bog.

The earliest traces of man are the Neolithic burial chambers found on the slopes of the hills, chief among which is Pentre Ifan cromlech. There is also evidence that the people of this period had axe-factories here, the products of which have been found over a wide area, including County Antrim and, in particular, Wessex. Although the sites of the factories have not been located, there would appear to have been two centres of production. The one produced axes of spotted dolerite, the same as that found among the foreign stones at Stonehenge, and the other used rhyolitic tuff which probably came from the eastern end of the range.

Men of the Bronze Age followed the trackway along the ridge of the hills on their way from Salisbury Plain to Ireland, in pursuit of copper and gold in the Wicklow Hills. Those who died on the long journey were buried where they fell, in round barrows or cairns along the ridgeway. The summit of Foel Drygarn (SN 157336), 'the hill of three cairns', is crowned by three Bronze Age burials, marked by the largest cairns in West Wales.

Stone circles are thought to belong to this period, of which there is only one example in Pembrokeshire, at Gors Fawr, and so are standing stones, of which over seventy have been identified along with an alignment of eight stones at Parc y Meirw.

Iron Age hill forts occupy prominent sites at Foel Drygarn, surrounding the Bronze Age cairns, and on Carn Ingli. The less formidable defences of Carn Alw are compensated by the presence of a *chevaux-de-frise*. Hut sites and enclosures within and around the defensive settlements suggest a sizeable pastoral population before and after the dawn of the Christian era.

In the *The Mabinogion* it is stated that Pwyll, prince of Dyfed, came to meet his nobles 'at Presseleu', when they urged him to take a wife so as to ensure his succession. Another tale tells how Arthur and his knights pursued the legendary wild boar, Twrch Trwyth, across the Presely Hills until it stood its ground at Cwm Cerwyn and slew four of the knights. Arthur is commemorated in the names of several of the outcrops, such as Bedd Arthur, 'Arthur's grave', Carn Arthur, 'Arthur's cairn' and Cerrig Meibion Arthur, 'the cairns of the sons of Arthur'.

For long, therefore, people have 'lifted their eyes unto the hills' for support, spiritual or material, for signs of weather, or to read what they could in their mood, that changes from season to season, and from hour to hour. The strange sanctity that caused men to transport more than eighty pillars of stone, weighing some 250 tons, from here to Stonehenge, still presides over these hills.

To follow the ancient trackway along the length of the hills when the purple heather and the gorse of pure gold form a carpet fit for kings, and when the air is sweet with wild thyme and the lark's enduring song, is to know something of that strange sanctity.

The trackway has been variously described, or marked on maps, as Roman Road, Robbers' Road, *Via Flandrica* or Flemings' Way, in a misguided effort to explain its origins. It was trodden by man 5,000 years ago, and it was used, until comparatively recent times, by the drovers who drove their cattle along this route out of Pembrokeshire towards the Midlands and Smithfield market.

A section of the trackway may be followed to the best advantage by turning off the A478 road at Pwll-glas (SN 181333) and following the minor road to Llainbanal (SN 168333), near where cars may be left in a lay-by. The suggested route terminates at Bwlch Gwynt (SN 074322), where it could be started, and where there are car-parking facilities.

At Croes Fihangel (SN 165332), 'Michael's Cross', a Bronze Age barrow was recently excavated and yielded five cinerary urns contain-

Presely ponies in winter (*B. R. Munt*)

ing the cremated remains of persons who lived, and died here, around 3,000 years ago.

Above Croes Fihangel rises Foel Drygarn (SN 157336) consisting of rhyolitic lava and volcanic ash of the Fishguard Volcanic Series. It is surmounted by a large hill fort that is divided into three contiguous enclosures, each defended by a single unditched rampart. There are over two hundred hut sites that suggest a considerable occupation, and finds from excavation appear to date from the first century BC. Within the fort are the three large Bronze Age cairns that gave the hill its name.

At Garn Ferched (SN 153330), 'the cairn of the daughters', a small Bronze Age barrow lies beside the trackway.

Carn Menyn (SN 142324) was a source of the bluestones of Stonehenge. In 1923 Dr H. H. Thomas of the Geological Survey was able to show that the three main varieties of foreign stones found at Stonehenge, namely spotted dolerite, spherulitic rhyolite and an altered volcanic ash, could be matched exactly with outcrops of igneous rocks in the Presely Hills, and that the only locality where the three types occurred in close proximity was in the area between the summits of Foel Drygarn and Carn Menyn. More than 80 stones were transported to Salisbury Plain, most of them spotted dolerite from the southern side of Carn Menyn and from Carn y Ddafad Las (SN 148329). Three were unspotted dolerite from the south side of Carn Menyn; 5 were volcanic ash from Foel Drygarn, and 4 white-speckled rhyolites from Carn Alw. Their columnar shape is due to natural fracture owing to frost action, and stones of a similar size and shape to the Stonehenge bluestones still break off in the hills and tumble down into the screes.

Carn Alw (SN 139337), to the north of Carn Menyn, is a small hill fort with a single rampart, the entrance to which is guarded by a well-defined *chevaux-de-frise*, comprising an area in which stones are set up on end so as to prevent the approach of an enemy, particularly on horseback. There are traces of field systems and stock enclosures around the outcrop. The dark blue, white-speckled rhyolitic rock of the outcrop provided four of the bluestone pillars for Stonehenge.

At Carn Arthur (SN 135323), 'Arthur's cairn', a boulder balanced precariously on another is said to mark the grave of King Arthur, although this is also claimed to be at Bedd Arthur (SN 131325), 'Arthur's grave', where twelve stones are arranged in an oval shape.

Carn Sian (SN 129321), 'Jane's cairn', to the south of Carn Bica, is claimed to have been the site of a chapel dedicated to St Silyn, or St Giles.

Carn Goedog (SN 123328), directly north of Carn Bica, appears in the popular Welsh ballad, *Y Mochyn Du*, 'the Black Pig', as the burial place of that unfortunate over-fed animal, that was solemnly conveyed thither in a horse-drawn hearse. A deep hollow to the west of the outcrop was caused by nivation, or erosion due to the action of snow. The small patchwork of fields on the open mountain, below Carn Goedog, is Hafod Tydfil (SN 116338), a relic of the system of transhumance. In summer, people moved with their livestock to the *hafod,* 'the summer dwelling', from the *hendre,* 'the old home', where they resided during the rest of the year. In this particular case, Hendre (SN 119366) lies directly north, at a lower level.

Cerrigmarchogion (SN 111323) is a name that may have an Arthurian connotation, for it means 'the crags of the knights'.

Foel Feddau (SN 103324), 'the hill of the graves', has a Bronze Age barrow on its summit, which is 1,531ft (467m).

Foel Cwm Cerwyn (SN 094312), to the south of the trackway, at 1,760ft (536m) above sea level is the highest point of the Presely Hills. It has four Bronze Age burials on its summit, one of which was excavated in 1806 and produced, among a quantity of charcoal and some

Foel Cwm Cerwyn, highest point of the Presely Hills (*B. R. Munt*)

unburnt bones, an encrusted urn. The steep-sided Craig-y-cwm (SN 098312) on the east side of the hill has a moraine deposited during the last glaciation at its lower end.

Bwlch Gwynt (SN 075321), 'the windy pass', is where the old road from Cardigan to Haverfordwest, the B4329, crosses the Presely Hills at a height of 1,325ft (405m). There are parking places that provide opportunities to enjoy the view, either to the north or to the south.

Foel Eryr (SN 066321), 'bare mountain', stands at 1,535ft (468m) and has a Bronze Age cairn on its summit. The path from the road at Bwlch Gwynt leads to a helpful viewfinder. On a clear day one may see Bardsey and Snowdonia to the north; the Carmarthenshire Vans to the east; Dunkery Beacon to the south, and to the west, the Wicklow Hills.

The trackway may be followed further, along the southern slope of Foel Eryr, and onward to join the road from New Inn to Fishguard at SN 043314.

Away from the trackway, there are other features of the Presely Hills that should be noted.

Freni Fawr (SN 204349) has Bronze Age cairns on its summit, which is 1,297ft (395m) above sea level. There is a local belief that a crock of gold lies buried on its slopes, but it is guarded by a terrifying 'phantom with tempest in his train'. A tale in *The Mabinogion* states that the Roman emperor Magnus Maximus, or Macsen Wledig, came to hunt on Freni Fawr and pitched his tent on the top of the hill, which was thereafter known as Cadair Facsen.

On the southern slopes, a pair of standing stones at Waun Lwyd (SN 158312) may be seen from the road at Glanrhyd (SN 153319).

The Gors Fawr stone circle (SN 134294) is the only circle of free-standing stones in the Presely Hills. It has sixteen stones, all less than 3 feet (1m) high, and a diameter of about 22 yards (20m), though it is not quite circular. Two taller outliers stand 440ft (135m) to the north-east, in the direction of Carn Menyn.

At Cerrig Meibion Arthur (SN 118310), 'the stones of the sons of Arthur', is a pair of stones standing, typically, with one thick, and blunt topped, and the other thin and tapering.

At Dyffryn (SN 059285) there is a cairn-circle, a ring of stones which enclosed, or was incorporated in, a Bronze Age barrow, a feature that is rare in this part of Wales.

On the north side of the hills, as the B4329 road approaches Tafarn-y-bwlch (SN 084337), a pair of standing stones may be seen away to the left, on 'the vacant wine-red moor'. Tafarn-y-bwlch was formerly a coaching inn, which had an Ivorites Club. The old drovers' road may be traced running south, to cross the ridgeway at SN 085322 and on to Rosebush and Maenclochog.

Bedd-yr-afanc (SN 109346), 'the monster's grave', is a wedge-shaped gallery grave of the Neolithic period that is exceptional in Wales and occurs elsewhere only in Ireland.

Carn Ingli (SN 062372), 'Ingli's mount', has been separated from the mass of the Presely Hills by the deep meltwater channel of the Gwaun Valley, cut when the Irish Sea glacier was wasting away. It is crowned by a massive hill fort that may have been begun around 300BC, but was occupied up to the fourth or fifth century AD. Its defensive ramparts are not easy to identify among the frost-shattered rocks that have tumbled down the slopes to form terraces and screes. The large number of hut circles and enclosures indicate a sizeable population during a period when defence was no longer so necessary.

Carnedd Meibion Owen (SN 092365) takes its name from the three sons of Owen ap Robert, who decided that they would not accept a gavelled share of their father's estate but rather that they should settle their patrimony by physical combat. They retired to the cairn above their home, armed with cudgels of oak, and fought until nightfall, but none overcame the other. Their mother then persuaded the father to name one as his heir, and to dispatch the other two, one to the court of the king of Scotland and the other to serve the king of England, and only thus was peace restored in the family.

9
THE PEMBROKESHIRE COAST PATH

The Pembrokeshire Coast Path is 180 miles (290km) in length. It may be walked from one end to the other, which takes up to ten days to do, but most people prefer a more leisurely approach. This can be done by starting from a selected spot and returning there, or else by leaving the path at a point (indicated by FP in the following narrative) where there is access, usually by footpath, to the main road.

The Coast Path may be joined most conveniently at a place where there is an official car park (indicated CP) or which is accessible by car but has little or no parking space (indicated P).

The availability of overnight accommodation is indicated by A, but fuller particulars are available in the Pembrokeshire Coast National Park Authority's *Coast Path Accommodation*.

The route is covered by the Ordnance Survey 1:50,000 Landranger Series, maps 145 Cardigan, 157 St David's and Haverfordwest, and 158 Tenby, or by the 1:25,000 Pathfinder Series maps SN 04/14, SN 03/13, SM 83/93, SM 62/72, SM 82/92, SM 81/91, SM 70, SM 80/90, SR 89/99, SS 09/19 and SN 00/10. *The Pembrokeshire Coast Path* by John H. Barrett, published by the Countryside Commission, contains excerpts from the 1:25,000 Ordnance Survey maps to cover the length of the path and is an essential companion for the serious walker.

Poppit Sands to Fishguard

The Coast Path begins, or ends if you come the other way, beyond St

Dogmael's at Poppit Sands (CPA), where there is a youth hostel. It travels along the slope above the estuary of the Teifi towards Cemais Head. The island across the inlet is Cardigan Island, a nature reserve of the West Wales Trust for Nature Conservation.

From Cemais Head to Newport there is a spectacular stretch of cliffs, formerly considered to be Silurian but now regarded as Ordovician grits and shales, layers of which, folded and faulted during the Caledonian earth movement, are well displayed at Cemais Head, Pen-yr-afr and Ceibwr (PA). Fulmars and choughs breed in the cliffs and grey seals haul out on the rocks and on beaches, sometimes in hundreds.

Pencastell, above Ceibwr, was an Early Iron Age promontory fort. Small ships used to discharge coal, culm and lime at Ceibwr, and a little contraband from time to time. There is a raised beach to the west of the bay.

Pwll-y-wrach (SN 103451), 'the witch's cauldron', is a collapsed blow-hole. The promontory fort at Castell Treruffydd has a single curved bank.

The path follows the 500ft contour from SN 092437 above Cell Howel and along the slopes of Foel Goch. Pwll Coch was the location of R. M. Lockley's *Seals and the Curragh* (1954) and here, thirty years later, was the hide-out of an international drug-smuggling gang that was finally brought to justice following *Operation Seal Bay* that has been described in a book of that name by Pat Molloy.

Carregedrywy (SN 047419) retains the forgotten element Edrywy which may have been the name of the district at one time. In early documents Newport (CPA) is referred to as Trefdraeth Edrywy.

Traeth Mawr (CP) at Newport is one of the finest and safest bathing beaches in Pembrokeshire, but somewhat marred by the failure of the authorities to implement the prohibition of car parking on the sands. There is a car park. Efforts are being made to arrest erosion of the sand dunes which has taken place in recent years. Adjoining the dunes is a nine-hole golf course with springy, wild thyme-scented turf.

Newport Bridge (CP), crossing the river Nevern, was completed in 1894; the stepping stones previously used at low tide may be seen above the bridge. Upstream, on the south bank, is Ffynnon Curig and, nearby, the site of Capel Curig. The parish church may have been dedicated to St Curig before the Normans changed the dedication to St Mary. Ffair Gurig used to be held on the saint's feast day, 16 June, but is now on 27 June. Immediately downstream, but now buried under a council rubbish dump, is the earliest trace of human settlement in north Pembrokeshire, where the finding of small flint implements indicate occupation by people of the Mesolithic period. Carreg Goetan Arthur Cromlech, now among houses at Pen-y-bont, is a Neolithic burial chamber with a massive capstone balanced on two of four upright pillars. Alongside the path on the south side of the river is a crescentic earthwork, marked 'Intrenchment' on the OS map, which may have been Iron Age; it is now partly destroyed to accommodate a tennis court.

Parrog (CP) may be the location of Trefdraeth, 'the town on the shore', before the Normans came and built their garrison town in front of the castle and called it *Novus burgus* or Newburgh and, later, Newport. The little harbour was busy with trade throughout medieval times. During the last century a hundred little vessels brought cargoes of coal, culm, lime and general merchandise each year, and there was a thriving ship-building industry. The sand bar at the mouth of the river hindered its development as a major port. The quay walls were built in 1825, along with five storehouses, one of which is now the Newport Boat Club and Sailing Centre. The last ketch came in on the tide in 1934 with a cargo of coal. The surviving limekiln, a rare double one, needs preservation.

The path passes in front of houses, now mostly holiday homes, to Cwm where a lifeboat house was built in 1884, and a lifeboat provided, following the wreck of the *Oline*, a Norwegian vessel, with the loss of five lives, the whole crew. A raised beach nearby was smoothed by over-riding ice of the Irish Sea glacier, and the bays along the coast have wave-cut platforms. Slate was quarried in the cliffs beyond Cwm and exported widely.

Aber Rhigian may have been the landfall for the Neolithic people who buried their dead at Cerrig y Gof (SN 037389), a unique circle of burial chambers.

Cwmyreglwys (P), 'the valley of the church', reminds one, at one moment, of Cornwall, at another, of Corfu. It has a fine sandy bathing beach when the tide is low, and is good for sailing. The west wall, with its vacant bellcote, is all that remains of the church of St Brynach after the great storm of 1859. The valley between Cwmyreglwys and Pwllgwaelod is a glacial meltwater channel that formerly separated Dinas Island from the mainland. *The Golden Year* and *Island Farmers* by R. M. Lockley tell of the author's life on Dinas Island Farm. A nature trail (P) around the headland has been prepared by the West Wales Trust for Nature Conservation. Razorbills, guillemots, great black-backed gulls and feral pigeons nest on Needle Rock and fulmars along the cliffs. Chough, raven, carrion crow, kestrel and buzzard are not un-

Old St Brynach's church at Cwmyreglwys, washed away by the sea save for the bell-coted west wall (B. R. Munt)

common. Squill, scabious and orchids flourish among the flora.

Pwllgwaelod (CP) has a sandy beach, and an inn, the *Sailors' Safety*. This was built to provide cheer for those who brought limestone for use on Island Farm from south Pembrokeshire to the limekiln opposite the inn. Pwllgwylog and Aber Bach are glacial overflow channels, and so is the Gwaun Valley which enters the sea at Lower Fishguard.

Fishguard Fort, at Castle Point, was built after the cutter *Black Prince* had held the town of Fishguard to ransom on 15 September 1779, but when invasion came in 1797 the garrison was able to do little about it. The path leaves the coast above the fort and follows the main road to Lower Fishguard, once the best harbour in north Pembrokeshire and famous for its pilchards and herrings. The Fishguard Bay Yacht Club stands at the end of the quay. The whole place was disguised as Llaregyb for the filming of *Under Milk Wood*.

The path hugs the coast to avoid the town of Fishguard (A). From Saddle Point is a splendid view of Fishguard Harbour, opened in 1906 to capture the Atlantic trade, but had to be content to become the port for southern Ireland.

Goodwick to St David's Head

A plaque on Goodwick beach commemorates the unconditional surrender of the French invaders of 1797. Goodwick Moor, now a

Strumble Head lighthouse, standing on the islet of Ynys Meicel (*Wales Tourist Board*)

Youth Hostel at Pwll Deri (*John L. Jones*)

nature reserve, may have been the site of the battle of Pwll Wdig in 1074, when Rhys ab Owain, king of South Wales, was killed.

Pentagonal dolerite columns appear at Penanglas. Maen Jaspis has veins of jasper of which, they say, the gates of paradise are made.

A memorial stone on Carreg Wastad Point (FP) records the last invasion of Britain by French renegades on the night of 22 February 1797. Some 1,400 men and 4 women climbed the steep ascent by the light of burning gorse bushes, carrying 2,000 stand of arms and rolling 47 barrels of gunpowder up the slope.

St Degan's Chapel was built in thankfulness for a safe landing. The rocks below bear the hoof prints of the saint's steed as he rode it out of the sea, and his sacred vest was preserved in the chapel until someone sold it to a passing stranger. Carreg Gybi is said to mark a landing by St Cybi, a Cornish saint commemorated at Caergybi (Holyhead) and elsewhere in Wales and Cornwall. The pillow-like masses of rock that appear along the coast are of lava that bubbled from a submarine volcano over the bed of the Ordovician sea. Ynys Onnen is of that lava. Ynys Meicel, on which Strumble Head lighthouse (P) was built in 1908, consists of Ordovician dolerite which was later intruded into the pillow lava.

Choughs and fulmars breed along this coast, and grey seals drop their young in caves and on stony beaches in the autumn.

Vapour trails high in the sky are transatlantic jets passing over homing beacon 'Green One'.

A YHA hostel stands over Pwll Deri (P) and beneath Garn Fawr, a major hill fort with multivallate defences, on the slopes of which is a corbelled hut and an oval enclosure, Ysgubor Gaer, 'the fort granary'.

A stone pillar above the bay was erected to the memory of Dewi Emrys (1879–1952), chaired and crowned bard, who immortalised Pwll Deri in a poem written in the local dialect. The last two lines of the poem form the inscription:

> A thina'r meddilie sy'n dwad ichi
> Pan foch chi'n ishte uwchben Pwllderi.
> 'Such are the thoughts that come to you as you sit above Pwll Deri.'

Trefasser was the birthplace of Asser, adviser, companion and biographer of King Alfred the Great, and Bishop of Sherborne when he died in 909.

The storm beach thrown up by the gale of 1859 at Aber Mawr (P) separates the sandy beach from the marshland, and a road that ran across the shingle bank was washed away by the sea earlier this century.

Remains of a submerged forest appear at very low tides, and periglacial deposits are exposed above the storm beach.

Castell Coch, 'red castle', occurs several times as a name for a promontory fort along this coast. The one on Penmorfa had an inner bank and an outer.

There are faint traces of a settlement on Ynys y Castell that may be early Christian. Here, at Bedd Bys Samson was buried the finger with which Samson raised the massive capstone of the Neolithic burial chamber, Carreg Samson, which is at Long House Farm nearby.

Little ships brought cargoes into Abercastle (P), particularly from Bristol: the village shop was called the 'Bristol Trader'. One of the limekilns remains in good shape, and there is also a granary in which corn was stored prior to export.

Another Castell Coch, beyond Ynys Deullyn, has two, or probably three, banks.

The ruin of a corn mill at Aberfelin, below the village of Trefin (A), inspired the poet and, later, archdruid, Crwys, one Sunday evening in 1918, to write one of the finest and most popular of Welsh lyrics, 'Melin Trefin'.

Porth-gain (CP), now a sleepy sea hamlet, once had a fleet of steam coasters and sailing ships exporting stone, slate and bricks. The stone was brought by rail from quarries in Ordovician igneous intrusions near Penclegyr, and crushed and graded into five hoppers before being sent, as road metal, as far afield as Somerset and Kent. Work ceased in 1931. Navigation marks on the headlands each side of the bay guided vessels into the harbour. The bulkhead of the *Carolina*, a Danish barque that sank off-shore in 1859, hangs in the bar of the Sloop Inn.

The path skirts Ynys Barry, which was insulated by a glacial meltwater channel. St Barré, or Finbar to the Irish, is said to have sailed from Traeth Llwyn to settle at an island retreat in the lake of Gouganebarra in County Cork. Traeth Llwyn is a beach of golden sand which may be approached on payment of a fee at Barry Island Farm. The steps were cut through glacial deposits by Italian prisoners during World War II.

Slate was quarried at the north end of Abereiddi Bay (CP) and exported in schooners until the quarry closed in 1904; local fishermen then blasted a passage to the sea to provide a safe anchorage for their boats in the 'Blue Lagoon'. Most of the slate, however, was taken by narrow-gauge railway to Porth-gain for export. The tower on Trwyn Castell was a navigation beacon. The Llanvirn shales of the Ordovician in Abereiddi Bay are notably fossiliferous, with the tuning-fork

Didymograptus bifidus and *Didymograptus murchisoni* predominant.

Caerau, meaning 'forts', is a formidable promontory fort with three ramparts, set back from the edge of the cliff. Yet another Castell Coch, above Aberdinas, has a double bank, but is much eroded. Below it is a blow-hole and a small slate quarry.

The path passes beneath Penberi, 'kite head' (FP). The red kite is no longer common here, but the peregrine falcon swoops on its prey, usually feral pigeons, along the coast. Penberi is an Ordovician doleritic monadnock, a remnant of the 600ft (180m) platform that resisted erosion and once stood out as an island when the sea level was much higher than it is today.

Ffosymynach, 'the monk's dyke', is an ancient trackway that crosses the St David's Peninsula from the western slopes of Penbiri to Ogof-y-ffos (SM 777244). Its origin and purpose are quite unknown, but it would appear to have a religious significance, such as the delineation of an area of sanctuary.

Carn Treliwyd, Carn Ffald, Carn Lleithir and Carn Llidi are plugs of Ordovician igneous rocks, or monadnocks, like Penberi. They stand above the surrounding countryside as isolated hills, or masses of rock, on account of their resistant nature.

From Penllechwen to St David's Head, the path follows a ridge of gabbro, or lava that had cooled slowly below the surface of the earth as it existed in Lower Ordovician times, getting on for 500 million years ago. Along and across the valley below, and on the slopes of Carn Llidi opposite, are traces of an Iron Age field system, revealing a continuity of agriculture extending over the last 2,000 years. An Iron Age fort (SM 727283) overlooks the valley. Evidence of an earlier occupation is provided by the Neolithic burial chamber, with capstone collapsed, known as Coetan Arthur, 'Arthur's quoit'. The belief that King Arthur had hurled a capstone, quoit fashion, from some distant spot was so prevalent that a burial chamber was often described, at one time, as 'a cromlech or Coetan Arthur'.

Clawdd y Milwyr, 'the warriors' dyke', was a massive rampart that provided a defence from landward for the promontory fort at Penmaendewi in which are the remains of eight circular huts of the Iron Age settlers.

Ptolemy, the Graeco-Egyptian astronomer, described Penmaendewi, in about 140AD, as *Octopitarum promontorium*, 'the promontory of the eight perils', referring to the off-shore rocks, the Bishops and Clerks. The lighthouse on the South Bishop rock was first lit in 1838 upon Queen Victoria's coronation day.

Ogof Grisial, 'crystal cave', at the north end of Clawdd y Milwyr, produces bright quartzspar, or St David's diamonds'.

Porth Melgan, a bay eroded in slates of the Lower Ordovician, has at its head a fine exposure of glacial deposits left by the Irish Sea glacier. It has a sheltered sandy beach.

Whitesand to St Ann's Head

Traeth Mawr, or Whitesand Bay (CPA), is a broad stretch of sand extending close on 2 miles (3km) at low water. Trwynhwrddyn, 'the little ram's nose', marks the line of a fault which runs out to sea between Ordovician shales and Cambrian flagstones. At low tide after tempestuous weather, the remains of a submerged forest appear at the northern end of the bay; antlers of red deer and the jaw bone of the brown bear found among the blackened tree stumps are deposited at the British Museum.

Bronze Age men sailed from here to Ireland, lured by copper and gold in the Wicklow Hills, having followed the ancient trackway from Salisbury Plain across the Presely Hills. Until recently OS maps showed this trackway as a 'Roman Road' or *Via Julia,* and indicated *Menapia,* a Roman station, at Whitesand, thus perpetuating a forgery perpetrated by Professor Charles Bertram (1723–65) in a fictitious itinerary of a fourteenth-century monk, Richard of Cirencester.

The remains of a small chapel at the north end of the beach is said to mark the spot where stood the miraculous stone on which St Patrick stood and saw Ireland 'notwithstanding the intervention of the mountains and sea', and thereupon set forth across the sea to convert the Irish.

Whitesand (A) is excellent for bathing and surfing but there are dangerous currents off parts of the beach and warning signs should be heeded. The St David's nine-hole golf course is on The Burrows, or Tywyn.

Porthselau (FP) is a small sandy beach, with rock pools, that connects with Whitesand at low water. Dorothy Jordan, the famous actress and mistress of the Duke of Clarence, later William IV, visited relatives at Treleddyn, above the bay.

St Justinian, a Breton saint, built himself a cell on Ramsey, and was murdered there. Determined, however, to be buried on the mainland, he walked across the Sound with his head under his arm. Around 1590 Bishop Vaughan built a chapel above his grave at Porthstinan (CP). Its bells were stolen by pirates whose boat was wrecked in the Sound, and it is said the chimes of the bells can be heard above the roar of the sea on stormy nights. The lifeboat house was erected in 1912 and a motor lifeboat launched in the following year. A previous lifeboat, the *Gem*, ran onto the The Bitches, the perilous reef in the Sound, and three of its crew were drowned. Boats cross from Porthstinan to Ramsey.

Ramsey is a detached fragment of the mainland platform. This, its Norse name, means Hrafn's island, but the Welsh name, Ynys Dewi, also survives. The island's caves and pebble beaches are the favourite breeding haunts of the grey seal on the Pembrokeshire coast.

Castell Heinif, a promontory fort, has a double rampart. Opposite The Bitches are traces of a copper mine. Porthmaenmelyn is the most westerly point on the mainland of Wales.

Porth Lisgi bears the name of an Irish raider who killed Boia, one-time enemy of St David. Carreg yr Esgob, 'the bishop's rock', is of intrusive Pre-Cambrian, or Dimetian, granite. From Carreg y Frân to Dinas Fach the cliffs expose Cambrian sedimentary rocks.

Porth Clais (CP) was 'the harbour of the *clas*', or monastic community of St David's. Stone from Caerfai and Caerbwdi was landed here and taken to build the cathedral, as was oak from Ireland, for the carved roof of its nave. King Arthur and his knights landed here from Ireland in pursuit of the legendary boar Twrch Trwyth.

St Non's Well is where Non lay down when her time came and gave birth to David. The well is arched over, with a recess for the reception of offerings for the cure of rheumatism and diseases of the eyes. St Non's Chapel became a cottage after the Reformation, with a garden of leeks. A retreat and chapel of the Passionist Fathers was established nearby in 1934.

Cambrian rocks of the Caerfai and Solva series are well exposed at Caerfai Bay (CPA). The purplish stone used in the building of the cathedral was quarried here, and the quarry was reopened in 1972 and enough stone taken to carry out repairs for the next fifty years. The ruins of a mill and a limekiln witness bygone activity.

The promontory fort at Penpleidiau has no less than four lines of defence against landward attack.

A massive fold in the purple Caerfai sandstone is faulted against green Solva sandstone on the west side of Caerbwdi Bay (FP). Stone was also taken from here to build the cathedral.

At Ogof-y-ffos, 'the dyke cave', is the southern end of Ffosymynach.

From Morfa Common the Smuggler Steps lead down to an old copper mine. Porth-y-rhaw (FP) has a ruined mill and brick buildings that formed part of the sewage works for the war-time St David's Airfield.

The folded and faulted rocks are Cambrian shales of the Menevia series, in which was found the 2ft (60cm) long trilobite *Paradoxides davidis* in 1862. The promontory fort to the east of the bay has interlocking banks to confuse the enemy.

Ogof Tybaco, 'tobacco cave', is below Llanunwas. There were hushed tales of false lights hung at the farmhouse 'to decoy the wandering mariner in order to benefit from his misfortune'. Small flints of Mesolithic hunters lie on the surface along the coast.

Trinity Quay at Solva was built in 1856 to handle and dress 3,500 tonnes of granite from Bodmin before transhipment to The Smalls for the building of a new lighthouse there. The previous one had been assembled at Solva in 1775 and fitted on iron columns that proved too rigid; they were replaced by oak pillars, the petrified stumps of which are still embedded in the remote rock.

Solva (CPA) is a village of unique character and attraction. As the main harbour in St Bride's Bay, it was busy with coastal trade up to the present century, and is now a popular yachting centre.

The coast path climbs the Gribin, a sharp ridge between two valleys eroded by meltwater channels. A promontory fort on the ridge has walling exposed on its north side.

The parish of St Elvis is named after the saint who baptised David but the church, now in ruins, was dedicated to St Teilo.

Traces of surface working for copper are visible at Dinas Mawr; efforts to mine silver there in the seventeenth century proved unsuccessful. Dinas Fach is overlooked by a promontory fort.

A nightingale was heard above Porth Mynawyd (FP) in 1948, despite St David's prayer to God that the bird's 'sweet tunings', which troubled him in his nightly orisons, should never again be heard within his diocese. Herons used to build their nests in the cliffs along here.

Pre-Cambrian volcanic rocks are exposed in the cliffs between Porth Mynawyd and Cwm Bach, where the Cambrian reappears. The coal measures begin at Newgale.

The submerged forest on Newgale Sands (CPA) appeared to King Henry II on his way to the shrine of St David in 1171, 'like a grove cut down, perhaps at the time of the Deluge'. The long stretch of sand is backed by a great ridge of pebbles, sorted out of the boulder clay in St Bride's Bay and built up by wave action and tidal currents. The inn is named after a former Duke of Edinburgh who called in 1882, but it then stood on the other side of the road. The pebble ridge has obstructed the brook and caused a marshy area to form in the valley.

Brawdy Brook, marked Brandy Brook by a wishful OS map marker,

Cliff farm, overlooking St Bride's Bay (B. R. *Munt*)

forms the western end of the linguistic divide between the Welshry of
north Pembrokeshire and 'Little England beyond Wales' to the south.

Near where Bathesland Water, a small stream, disappears into the
pebbles, is the site of a chapel built to mark the spot where the body of
St Caradog rested while its bearers sought shelter from a downpour of
rain. When they emerged they marvelled to find the silken pall and the
body of the saint, quite dry.

The coal measures are exposed along the coast as far as Musselwick,
except for interruptions of Ordovician Bala shales and Millstone Grit
around Druidston Haven. Coal was worked here from the fifteenth century up to 1905 when the Trefrân Cliff Colliery was closed. A red brick
stack on the edge of the cliff marks the westernmost mine of the Pembrokeshire Coalfield, which also stretches out under St Bride's Bay.

A quay and a pier built at Nolton Haven (CPA) in 1979 for the purpose of exporting coal and culm have long disappeared. The village of
Nolton, 'an old town', is a little inland.

Erratic boulders along the coast were brought from the St David's
Peninsula by glaciers and dropped as the ice melted.

A cliff path at Druidston Haven (FP) leads to a stretch of sand that reaches from Madoc's Haven, where St Madoc is said to have landed from Ireland, to Druidston Chins. Druidston, a hamlet away from the coast, takes its name from Alfred Drue who settled here early in the twelfth century.

Haroldston Bridge (SM 859154) is a natural arch. Black Point Rath is a promontory fort; *rath*, an Irish word, is used in mid-Pembrokeshire to describe an earthwork of indeterminate origin.

The Sleek Stone is a smooth monocline faulted on its north side. Layers of sandstone interbedded with blue-black shales of the coal measures at Broad Haven were subjected to intense folding during the Armorican earth movement.

The National Park Information Centre at Broad Haven specialises in matters relating to marine life and has, adjacent to it, a youth hostel which has facilities for the disabled.

Broad Haven (CPA) is a popular seaside resort with a wide sandy beach that extends into The Settlands bay at low tide.

Little Haven (CPA) lies in a small bay cut into the soft coal measures between headlands of more resistant sandstone. It was once busy with smacks and ketches taking coal away from the nearby collieries; nowadays in summer it is bright with boats and bathers. The Coast Path leads to The Point, with its panoramic view of St Bride's Bay from Ramsey to Skomer Island.

From Falling Cliff, where there are collapsed coal pits, to Foxes' Hole the rocks are Pre-Cambrian intrusive.

Goultrop, a Norse name meaning 'boar's bay', provides the only shelter from all weathers in St Bride's Bay and at one time had a lifeboat station. The slopes are hung with oakwood. Borough Head provides a splendid view of the full sweep of St Bride's Bay.

Howney Point Rath, covering about a ½ acre (¼ha) and protected by a double rampart, stands above Brandy Bay, the next bay to which is Dutch Gin. Seals haul out on the Stack Rocks off-shore.

Broadmoor Rath, between Foxes' Hole and Mill Haven (FP), is enclosed by a convex rampart and a ditch. The path changes colour as Pre-Cambrian rocks give way to the old red sandstone.

A small chapel at St Bride's Haven (PA) was washed away by the sea after it had been converted into a salt-house for curing herrings, and the herrings disappeared from the bay. Stone coffins appear in the eroded cliff face, near the limekiln. The church is dedicated to St Bride of Kildare, a lady saint who has more dedications in Wales than all the other Irish saints together; her cult was probably brought by Irish col-

Emmet Rock at Broad Haven (*B. R. Munt*)

onisers of the fifth and sixth centuries. The house on the hill, once known as Hill, was built by William Edwardes, Lord Kensington. It later became the Kensington Hospital and is now a country hotel.

The Nab Head was an important clifftop settlement during the Mesolithic period. Finds include small flint implements, pierced shale discs, and wood-cutting tools of the Maglemosian culture. Tower Point Rath is a promontory fort with a triangular enclosure defended by a curved rampart. Fulmars breed in the cliffs, and prostrate broom spreads close to the ground.

Ordovician shales intrude at Musselwick (FP). From there as far as the Deer Park, rocks of the Skomer Volcanic Series contain Skomerite and Marloesite.

At Martin's Haven (CP), scolding stonechats sound just like stone hitting stone, and yellowhammers plead for a little-bit-of-bread-and-no-cheese. The West Wales Trust for Nature Conservation has an information centre at Lockley Lodge, with particulars of the boat service to Skomer Island.

The Coast Path pierces a high stone-built wall erected across the neck of the peninsula by Lord Kensington to provide a Deer Park. There is no account of deer being brought here, but the name persists. An earlier rampart of earth and stone isolated the peninsula some 2,000 years ago to form the largest promontory fort in Wales. The coastguard lookout commands a view of St Bride's Bay and the islands. Wooltack

Point overlooks Jack Sound through which the tide rips at 6 knots (11km/h). The Deer Park is covered in thrift, sea campion, heather, gorse and bracken, with prostrate broom on the cliff edges.

From The Anvil to the southern end of Marloes Sands, the rocks are Silurian with the exception of the Horse Neck which, like Gateholm, is old red sandstone. The Iron Age rampart comes almost to the cliff edge at Renney's Slip.

Marloes Rath, above Watery Bay, has a triple line of bank and ditch for defence. In 1837 the packet *Albion,* having struck a rock in Jack Sound, ran ashore in the next bay with passengers for Dublin and 180 pigs; they say the pigs swam ashore and provided rashers for Marloes breakfast tables.

Gateholm, Norse for 'goat island', is separated from the mainland at low tide. On its undulating surface are traces of 130 rectangular huts and 8 enclosures, which may be the remains of an early Christian monastic settlement.

Marloes Sands (FP) extends over 1 mile (1½km) below tall Silurian cliffs which were tilted into a vertical position during the Armorican earth movement at the close of the Carboniferous period. Silurian fossils here have much in common with those of Nova Scotia, for in Silurian times North America was near and had not begun to drift westward. At Red Cliff, at the south end of Marloes Sands, the old red sandstone reappears and extends to cover the whole of the Dale Peninsula (A).

From West Dale Bay (FP), the Ritec Fault runs the length of Milford Haven and across to the Ritec at Tenby and, under Carmarthen Bay, to the Gower Peninsula, which it nearly separates from the mainland. The Dale Peninsula was an island in pre-glacial times, until material released by the retreating ice formed the Dale Valley.

Great Castle Head Rath has two curved ramparts. Above Long Point the Royal Naval Radar and Meteorological School was established during the last war. Fragments of worked flints indicate Mesolithic occupation above Welshman's Bay.

St Ann's Head (FP) was the southern limit of the last glaciation and boulders brought from the Lake District and Scotland by the Irish Sea glacier are found as far south as here. The melting ice caused the sea level to rise, drowning the pre-glacial valley that is now Milford Haven.

When he landed at Mill Bay in 1485 Henry Tudor is said to have built a chapel dedicated to St Ann. It was later demolished and its site used as a base for a lighthouse built in 1714.

Cobbler's Hole, below the foghorn, displays colourful layers of rocks that were folded and faulted during the Armorican earth movement. The Neopolitan-cake effect is, of course, best seen from the sea.

At Mill Bay a little before sunset on Sunday 7 August 1485, Henry Tudor landed with a mixed army of 2,000 men and set off, with all speed, to Bosworth.

Milford Haven

A fort built at West Blockhouse (FP) in 1580, and another at East Blockhouse (SM 842028), represented the first attempts at fortifying Milford Haven. The present two-storied barrack with six guns en barbette was built in 1857 at a cost of £45,000 to plans prepared by Lieutenant Charles George Gordon RE, later of Khartoum fame. An open battery was built on higher ground in 1900 and was manned until 1950. Transit marks here and further on guide ships along the deep-water channel in the Haven.

Watwick Bay lies in a downfold so that both sides of the bay dip towards the middle. A white diamond sign was used in connection with the war-time anti-submarine barrage.

Above Castlebeach Bay, which has a ruined limekiln and the remains of the lime-burner's cottage, is an Iron Age fort which has recently been excavated.

Dale Fort was built in 1856. Since 1947 it has been a Field Studies Council Field Centre.

The Coast Path follows the road from Dale Fort through Dale village (PA), a popular yachting centre, to the Gann estuary. Gravel was taken from here to build the Dale Airfield during World War II and the sea has flooded the excavated areas. Winter bird visitors include spoonbill and little egret.

Monk Haven (FPA) was the harbour of the monastery of St Ishmael's. A road leading from here to St David's was known as the Welsh Way. The wall across the beach is eighteenth century.

Great Castle Head has a large promontory fort defended by a single rampart, and there is a similar enclosure at Little Castle Head.

Sandy Haven (P) is said to have been the landing place of the Flemings sent by Henry I in 1108 to settle in mid-Pembrokeshire.

The fort on Stack Rock was completed in 1867 and equipped with twenty-three guns. South Hook Fort was built two years earlier.

The Esso Oil Refinery, opened in 1960, closed in 1984. The long jetty was built out to reach the pre-glacial deep-water channel, and dredged deeper to allow passage for tankers of 300,000 tonnes. The jetty to the east is connected by pipelines to the Amoco refinery further inland.

Gelliswick Bay (CP) has a sandy beach and a sailing club. Hubberston Fort, above the bay, was equipped with twenty-eight guns when completed in 1865; it was altered in 1900 to include an open battery. Below it are the offices and pier of the Milford Haven Conservancy Board.

The coast path passes through the town of Milford (A) and returns to the coast at the Gulf Refinery, which opened in 1968. It joins the road at Hazelbeach (A) and on to Llanstadwell. Thomas Balymore, the vicar of St Tudwal's, received forty shillings for accommodating Richard II on his way to Ireland in 1394.

After passing through Neyland and crossing the Cleddau Bridge to Pembroke Dock (A), the path travels along the north bank of the Pembroke River to Pembroke (A) and Monkton, where it leaves the main road and passes the Pembroke Power Station, completed in 1975 at a cost of £105 million. Its output of 2,000 megawatts is carried by 400kV power lines across South Wales to Bristol and the Midlands.

The Texaco Oil Refinery, opened in 1964, is the only refinery south of the Haven. The BP Ocean Terminal was connected to the company's refinery at Llandarcy, near Swansea, by buried pipeline when it was built in 1961. Its offices were concealed inside Popton Fort, completed in 1864, and its tank farm was placed at Kilpaison, on Angle Bay. The terminal closed in 1985.

Angle Bay is a winter resort of waders and wildfowl. The path passes the village of Angle (CPA) to Angle Point and on past the Angle lifeboat station. A small chapel stood above Chapel Bay and there was another chapel at West Angle Bay (CP). The fort on Thorn Island, completed in 1859, has been converted into an hotel.

Rat Island to Amroth

Overlooking Rat Island is East Blockhouse, built in 1580 and later remodelled. Skomer Neck Camp, above Sheep Island, is a promontory fort defended by a single bank; another stands above West Pickard Bay.

Freshwater West (P) has a long stretch of sand, but bathing is dangerous. Sand dunes have covered Bronze Age burials and surrounded Devil's Quoit burial chamber. Over 7,000 flints have been found on a Mesolithic site at Little Furzenip. The only material evidence left by the Norse in Pembrokeshire was a leaden tablet found here. A calvary commemorates those who fell in World War I.

There is no access to the coast between Gupton Burrows and Flimston, over the Castlemartin Tank Ranges, and so the path follows the road through Castlemartin to Merrion Camp and turns right at SR 932971 for the coast.

On firing days, announced in the local papers and in Bosherston Post office, the exclusion extends as far as a gate above Broad Haven at SR 976937 and one has to follow the road to Sampson Cross (SR 965964) and turn right for Bosherston (CPA).

The Green Bridge of Wales (SR 925944) is a natural arch of limestone created by marine erosion; when the arch collapses, as it will one day, a stack will be left, like Eligug Stack nearby. Eligug is a local name for the guillemot, which densely populates the ledges of the Stack, in company with razorbills, kittiwakes and fulmar petrels. The top of the Stack has a tousled growth of tree mallow.

Flimston Castle, is a promontory fort with multiple defences, behind which are traceable a number of hut hollows. Tradition has it that the Flemings sent to Pembrokeshire in 1108 landed here: Flimston means 'Flemings' settlement'. The natural harbour was used to load limestone quarried locally. Crocksydam also has an Iron Age fort, with a single rampart and ditch; pottery found here showed that the site was occupied up to the fourth century AD.

Recent discoveries have revealed that caves, which are now high in the cliffs, were occupied during Neolithic times, or even earlier.

The Castle, a promontory fort on Buckspool Down, has a single rampart and ditch and appears to have been occupied during the second century AD.

From a National Park car park at Bosherston, a path leads to the Bosherston Lily Pools that were formed, in calcareous marls, when three streams were dammed at the end of the eighteenth century, and now form part of the Stackpole National Nature Reserve. In the late spring and early summer the lakes are covered with white water lilies, beneath which lurk perch, roach and tench, and many a hungry pike. Legend states that it was from these waters that a hand reached forth to receive King Arthur's sword, Excalibur.

A path around the western lake proceeds along the eastern lake, passing an eight-arched bridge and the site of Stackpole Court and on towards Stackpole village. Broad Haven has a fine stretch of sand and on its north-west side is a raised beach. On the landward side of the sand dunes behind the bay is a thicket of sea-buckthorn.

At SR 967930, and nestling half way down the cliff is St Govan's Chapel. St Govan of Dairinis, it is believed, landed here, having sailed in his curragh from county Wexford, and built a cell in thanksgiving for a safe landing. When marauders came he hid in a cleft in the rock by the altar, into which one may squeeze and wish a wish, and when his time came, he was buried in the sanctuary. The bell, of solid silver, was stolen from its bellcote by pirates, but the sea raged in fury at the sacrilege and sank their boat. Sea nymphs restored the bell from the sea bed, and set it in a rock that rings out when struck, beside the saint's holy well. The chapel has been carefully renovated by the National Park Authority for which it received a Prince of Wales Award in 1982.

A car park and picnic site has been provided by the National Park Authority on the cliff top above the chapel, from which there are spectacular views of the tall limestone cliffs that stretch like great fortress walls to the east and to the west. Caves high in the cliff face were occupied during the Stone Age by men who hunted in forests that now lie beneath the sea.

Huntsman's Leap, to the west of St Govan's, is a deep chasm across which a huntsman leapt, and then died of shock. Bosherston Mere consists of connected blowholes that blow cold geysers during sou'westerly gales.

Broad Haven (CP) was the estuary of three converging streams until a sandbar and an eighteenth-century dam impeded their flow and thus formed the Bosherston Pools. Stackpole Court was rebuilt in 1735 by John Campbell but demolished by his descendant Lord Emlyn, later Earl Cawdor, in 1962. Traces of a Bronze Age settlement have come to light during excavation on Stackpole Warren, and cremated remains were found beneath Devil's Quoit, a standing stone.

From Stackpole Head there is a splendid vista of the coast from St Govan's Head to Old Castle Head and Caldey. Griffith Lort's Hole is a reminder that the Stackpole estate was the Lort's before Alexander Campbell of Cawdor married the heiress.

Barafundle Bay has a sandy beach which may only be approached from the Coast Path. Here the old red sandstone takes over from the carboniferous limestone.

Stackpole Quay (CP) lies in a cove carved from a quarry from which limestone was exported from the little quay built for the purpose.

Greenala has unusually strong defences for so small an enclosed area.

Freshwater East's wide stretch of sand, backed by dunes, has been marred by uncontrolled holiday development. Intrusions of Silurian and Ordovician interrupt the old red sandstone. An Iron Age fort above the north end of the beach, which has survived for 2,000 years, is in danger of being destroyed by human erosion.

On the coast path above Manorbier beach (*Wales Tourist Board*)

Manorbier Castle stands sentinel above the beach, and guards the village of Manorbier (CPA). Above Priest's Nose is a collapsed burial chamber known as the King's Quoit. The promontory fort at Old Castle Head has traces of hut circles.

At Skrinkle Haven steep Armorican folds, truncated by the 200ft (60m) wave-cut platform, have left vertical bedding, as they have done elsewhere along the coast, especially between Freshwater East and Lydstep. The tall arch has been formed by the pincer action of the waves eating into the up-ended layers of limestone.

The carboniferous limestone outcrops vertically again at Whitesheet Rock, which stands above a raised beach cut when the sea level was 20ft (6m) higher than it is today.

Lydstep Point, a National Trust property, has a nature trail prepared by the West Wales Trust for Nature Conservation. Lydstep Cavern should be visited at low tide. Lydstep House was the home of the first Viscount St David's early this century. From Lydstep Haven a sharp syncline reaches out to sea and is eroded to form Caldey Sound.

On either side of Proud Giltar (FP) blow-holes are connected to large caves. St Teilo is said to have been born at, or near, Penally.

A post-glacial bank, extending from Giltar Point to the South Cliffs at Tenby, is the nucleus of the sand dunes known as The Burrows. This bank led to the silting of the Ritec valley so that ships could no longer sail up to Gumfreston and St Florence. The accumulation of sand was accelerated by the building of an embankment across the estuary in 1820 in order to reclaim land. The railway line to Pembroke was laid along the embankment in 1863. The Coast Path cuts across The Burrows to join the main road at Penally (PA) and then follows the railway line in to the town of Tenby, thus avoiding the mile (1½km)-long stretch of sand dunes and the Tenby Golf Course. It then leaves Tenby along Waterwynch Lane. Charles Norris, the artist, whose drawings are exhibited at the Tenby Museum, built a house at Waterwynch (FP) in 1821 on the site of an old grist mill. The next stream, in Lodge Valley, empties on to an expansive wave-cut platform.

Above the knife-back promontory of Monkstone Point (FP), on 16 May 1970, following negotiations extending over the previous seventeen years, the Pembrokeshire Coast Path was officially opened by the celebrated broadcaster, Wynford Vaughan-Thomas, who described it as a 'a shining girdle around the county'.

Dwarf oaks hang down the cliffs beyond Monkstone. Unexpected growths of *Cotoneaster simonsii* grow on the slopes above the path, which travels through woodland towards Saundersfoot and leaves the resort along The Strand, formerly Railway Street, where coal-carrying trams used to be drawn, first by horses and, from 1915, by steam locomotive, from the surrounding collieries to Saundersfoot harbour.

When the tide is low, one may walk along the sands almost all the way to Amroth.

Coal was carried in carts to Coppet Hall and loaded on to small vessels, of which as many as thirty would be beached at the same time. Beyond Coppet Hall are a couple of adits, or horizontal mine shafts, and the path follows the tramway that connected the Kilgetty colliery and the Stepaside ironworks with Saundersfoot. Thin seams of coal appear in the cliff face. The woodland forms part of the grounds of Hean Castle, built by Charles Vickerman in 1876 and purchased in 1899 by Sir William Thomas Lewis, the first Lord Merthyr. The name is a corruption of *hen gastell*, 'old castle', and refers to a prehistoric earthwork.

In August 1943 Wiseman's Bridge (CPA) was the scene of a rehearsal for the beach landings in Normandy the following June, watched, it is said, by the Prime Minister, Winston Churchill.

Amroth, formerly known as Earwere, appears to have been originally a Norse settlement. Near the church is the site of a Norman motte. The castellated house near the beach and known as Amroth Castle was built around 1800. At low water, blackened stumps of trees mark the submerged part of the ancient forest of Coedrath and among them have been found petrified hazel nuts, a Roman coin, and flint arrow heads used in the chase 10,000 years ago.

The Pembrokeshire Coast Path ends, or begins, near the New Inn, at the boundary of the former county of Pembroke.

10
EXPLORING BY CAR

For those who do not wish to walk the Coast Path there is a road that follows the coast for most of the way. This could be undertaken all in one by car as a leisurely day's journey, or it could be taken in sections. Other parts of the National Park, and contiguous areas, may also be explored by car.

The Coast

Beginning at the northern limit of the National Park, at Poppit Sands, take the minor road to Cipyn and follow towards Moylegrove. Caerau, at SN 124454, is a large Iron Age fort with three concentric embankments, causing the road to sweep round its contours. The site was believed to be haunted by a white lady and many a man was led astray, to wander until cock-crow, it was said, except for a drunken fisherman from St Dogmael's who was able to guide himself home by the pole star.

There are splendid views along this road over St George's Channel and Cardigan Bay.

At Moylegrove turn right for Ceibwr Bay.

Return to the coast road and proceed towards Newport. At SN 066419 the road leads to Newport Sands, crossing the golf course. Return to SN 063414: turn right, and right again at SN 067415 for Newport Bridge. The coast road joins the A487 as you enter the ancient borough of Newport, where there is a National Park Information

Centre at Bank Cottage, Long Street, with a car park opposite, and shops, inns, restaurants and art galleries. A road runs down to the Parrog, where the sea comes up to the quay walls when the tide is high.

The A487 leaves Newport for Dinas. At SN 019388 a narrow road leads off to Cwmyreglwys and at SN 012389 another takes one to Pwllgwaelod.

From the hill running down towards Fishguard there is a fine distant view of the town and its environs. At SM 974374 the road leaves the National Park as the towns of Fishguard and Goodwick were excluded when the boundaries of the Park were drawn.

At SM 963376 a pull-in viewpoint above Fishguard Fort overlooks the bay and Fishguard Harbour rail and cross-channel boat terminus, with Goodwick and Pen-caer beyond. The imposing building above the harbour is the Fishguard Bay Hotel.

The road winds down to Lower Fishguard. It takes a sharp right turn at the Dinas Arms for the quay, where *Under Milk Wood* was filmed and where the Fishguard Bay Yacht Club is situated. It goes straight on, after the turn for Fishguard town, for a short distance, to the Workshop Gallery, which has an art exhibition located within an arts and crafts complex.

A steep hill leads to the town of Fishguard. A memorial to Jemima Nicholas, the Welsh heroine, stands beside St Mary's Church, approaching Fishguard Square. At the Royal Oak, it is claimed, the treaty was signed following the last invasion of Britain by the French in 1797: in fact, the French only came there to seek terms of surrender.

There is little evidence of early settlement in the town itself. Even the parish church has been completely rebuilt, on the site of a previous one that was 'scarcely distinguishable from the adjacent houses'.

The stone circle on Penslade was erected for the ceremonies of the Gorsedd of Bards when the Royal National Eisteddfod of Wales was held at Fishguard on its first visit to Pembrokeshire in 1936. Each pillar was presented by one of the surrounding parishes. When it came again, fifty years later, the site was inadequate and another circle was erected in Lota Park.

The Fishguard Music Festival, first held in 1970, comprises a series of concerts and recitals by artistes of international repute, a poetry recital and art exhibitions and is, by now, one of the leading festivals in Wales.

Bear right at Fishguard Square to follow the road towards Goodwick, crossing the Parrog, on the seaward side of which is a tablet commemorating the surrender of the French troops on Goodwick Sands, at low tide, on Friday 24 February 1797. Goodwick Moor on the left hand side, though now partly drained, is a nature reserve.

After crossing the railway bridge, turn left.

The road from Goodwick climbs to Stop and Call (SM 949381) and carries on to Llanwnda where the bellcoted church has a number of cross-incised stones and one, built into the church wall, bearing a face which may represent the Virgin Mary. Carreg Wastad Point on the coast below, where the French landed in 1797, is marked by a memorial stone erected on the headland during the centenary commemoration. The road passes Trehowel Farm (SM 918399) which the French commandeered as their headquarters, and here *chef de brigade*, William Tate, delivered his sword to Lord Cawdor and signed articles of capitulation, which have never been found.

At Trefasser (SM 895379), birthplace of Asser, adviser to King Alfred and later Bishop of Sherborne, the road turns off to Pwll Deri, where there is a youth hostel and a stone pillar commemorating the Welsh poet Dewi Emrys among whose works is a memorable poem to Pwllderi. Garn Fawr, rising behind, has a massive hill fort of the Iron

The ruined mill at Trefin (*B. R. Munt*)

Age with multivallate defences and hut sites.

Returning to Trefasser, the road proceeds along the coast and leads, with a slight diversion, to the Tregwynt Woollen Factory at SM 894348.

A narrow lane takes one to Aber Mawr from where a submarine cable was laid to Ireland in 1883.

Follow the road to Mathry, set on a hill, from which there are panoramic views of the surrounding countryside. Return to the coast at Abercastle. Carreg Samson burial chamber is above Abercastle, in a field adjoining Long House Farm (SM 846336). The road proceeds towards Trevine and on past the ruined mill at Aberfelin (SM 834324), which inspired the Welsh poet Crwys to write the famous poem *Melin Trefin.*

The church at Llanrhian, dedicated to St Rheian, has a thirteenth-century tower but the rest was rebuilt in the middle of the nineteenth century. The road turns off here for Porth-gain. Return to Llanrhian and follow the coast road to SM 809306 where there is an offshoot to Abereiddi. Return again to the coast road and proceed towards St David's.

At Capel y Gwrhyd (SM 767275) there once stood a chapel which had an arch bearing the figure of St David with his arms outstretched: 'gwrhyd' is the Welsh for a fathom, and the original meaning of the word 'fathom' was the reach of the outstretched arms. Just beyond is Rhodiad y Brenin, 'where the king walked by'. Rhodiad Chapel, established in 1784, was the mother chapel of the Congregationalists in the St David's Peninsula.

Dowrog Moor, on the left, is a nature reserve of the West Wales Trust for Nature Conservation. At one time it was known as Tir-y-pererinion, 'the pilgrims' land', and is said to have been granted by Rhys ap Tewdwr, prince of South Wales, to the bishops of St David's for the use of pilgrims making their devotions at the shrine of the saint.

The road turns off at SM 758261 for Whitesand Bay, or Porth Mawr.

There is no road round the St David's Peninsula but lanes lead from St David's to St Justinian's, or Porthstinan (the lifeboat station and embarkation point for Ramsey) to Porth-clais (the harbour of the monastic community and the cathedral) and to Caerfai.

Pilgrims have made their way to St David's for the last 1,500 years, and it is no less a place of pilgrimage today. Two visits to St David's equalled one to Rome, which was convenient for the Irish saints who passed this way on their route to the Continent.

There is a National Park Information Centre at the City Hall and

Rickett's Head, at the south end of Newgale Sands (*B. R. Munt*)

there are shops, hotels, inns and some good eating places.

The road leads from St David's to Solva with inns and shops, and continues to Newgale and along its wide stretch of sands.

Tangible evidence of the Pembrokeshire Coalfield appears in the form of a red-brick chimney-stack on the edge of the cliff at SM 856197. The coal was taken to Nolton Haven for export.

The coast road bears right by the chapel at Nolton Haven and dips down to Druidston Cross. It then passes the little Haroldston Church and goes down Haroldston Hill to Broad Haven which has a National Park Information Centre, hotels and a shop. The road travels along the sea front before proceeding to Little Haven with inns and a village shop.

The road leaves Little Haven for Talbenny and, after passing the wartime Talbenny airfield, turns right for St Bride's Haven. It then continues south until it meets the B4327 and crosses the serpentine Mullock Bridge. A fanciful legend maintains that Sir Rhys ap Thomas crouched under this while Henry Tudor passed over on his march from Dale to Bosworth; he had promised King Richard that Henry should not enter the land except over his body.

After crossing the bridge, the road branches to the right to pass through the village of Marloes, formerly a village of fishermen and their families, on to Martin's Haven, from which boats cross to Skomer Island and Skokholm.

Return to Marloes and, after leaving the village, bear right and after a little way join the road to Dale. Cars may park on the verge, facing Dale Roads, with a view up the Milford Haven Waterway, and there are places for refreshments. A one-way road takes one to SM 806057 at which a detour may be made to St Ann's Head, where there are splendid views of the Haven and the off-shore islands.

Return to pass Dale Castle and to join the road to Haverfordwest. Beyond Mullock Bridge follow the road leading to St Ishmael's. The church, near Goose Green, may be on the site of a monastery that stood above Monk Haven. Follow the road through the village and beyond Bicton turn right. At SM 854085, a lane leads down to Sandy Haven, where Graham Sutherland first found inspiration in Pembrokeshire.

The road skirts the top of Sandy Haven Pill and passes by Herbrandston towards Hubberston. The oil refinery to the north is Amoco. At Lodge Farm, SM 886073, keep right for Hubberston and enter the town of Milford by crossing Hakin Bridge, where there is a memorial to the first, and unexpected, royal visit to the town, on 13 September 1821, when George IV on his return from Ireland encountered a severe storm and was brought ashore. The Lord Nelson Hotel in Hamilton Terrace, formerly Front Street, overlooks Milford Docks and the Fishermarket: here Nelson made his famous speech in which he said that he considered Milford Haven and Trincomalee the finest harbours he had ever seen. At St Katherine's Church turn left, and at Prioryville turn right for Neyland, passing through Castle Hill Pill. On the eastern bank once stood Castle Hall, home of Robert Fulke Greville, which was demolished in 1934 to make way for the armaments depot at Newton Noyes.

The village of Waterston has the Gulf Oil Refinery, built on its doorstep in 1968.

The grassy mound in a field on the left at SM 945066 is part of Scoveston Fort built in 1865 at a cost of £45,000 to provide defence against attack from landward. Scoveston point-to-point races are held here.

Neyland became the terminus of the South Wales Railway, later the Great Western Railway, in 1856, and was known as New Milford. Brunel had thoughts of promoting it as a great port and his *Great Eastern*, then the largest vessel ever built, at about 20,000 tonnes, was anchored here: Brunel Avenue and Great Eastern Terrace are memorials. After circling Neyland, join the new road leading to the Cleddau Bridge. This was completed in 1975 after a delay of seven years owing to the collapse of a section of the box girder structure; the cost meanwhile had rocketed from £3 million to £18 million – which accounts for the relatively high toll charges. The road passes by Pembroke Dock and makes for Pembroke, where it arrives at Pembroke Bridge in the shadow of Pembroke Castle, the entrance to which is by the Barbican Gate in the main street. Here Henry Tudor, the founder of the Tudor dynasty, was born to the fourteen-year-old Margaret Beaufort on 28 January 1457. There are hotels, inns and shops in plenty at Pembroke.

Monkton, along the B4320, has few traces of its priory, except for the sanctuary which forms part of the chancel of the church.

The road proceeds through Hundleton and on towards Angle. To the right is the Pembroke Power Station and further along, the Texaco Oil Refinery.

At Speculation Inn (SM 947997) is the largest group of Bronze Age barrows in West Wales: cinerary urns found within the mounds indicate the burial of the cremated remains of people who travelled along the southern route to Ireland in search of copper and gold.

The road crosses Kilpaison Burrows, where there are the collapsed remains of a burial chamber, the Devil's Quoit. Angle Bay is on the right.

Turn right off the B4320 at SM 867018 for Angle and carry on to West Angle Bay, an embarkation point for Bronze Age traders on their way to Ireland.

Returning from West Angle Bay, turn right at SM 861030 and follow the B4320 to SM 884010 and turn right to join the B4319 for Castlemartin. The road crosses the sand dunes of Broomhill Burrows and Gupton Burrows. To the right is Freshwater West bay and sands: the remains of a submerged forest appears at certain low tides. Mesolithic flakes found in the area, Bronze Age barrows among the dunes, and Iron Age forts to the north of the bay indicate a continuation of settlement during prehistoric times.

At Castlemartin bear right to follow the B4319. At SR 932971, when there is no firing on the Castlemartin Ranges, a minor road leads off to the coast above the Green Bridge of Wales and Eligug Stack.

Return to the B4319 and proceed to Sampson Cross. At Sais's, or Saxon's, Ford nearby, the legend says three standing stones come together on Midsummer's Eve to dance the hay. Turn right for Bosherston and, when there is no firing on the range, follow the road to the edge of the cliff, where there is a car park above St Govan's Chapel.

Saundersfoot during the holiday season (*Countryside Commission*)

Return to Sampson Cross and follow the B4319 for a short distance before turning right at SR 970966 for Stackpole, a village built to serve Stackpole Court, erected in 1735 on the site of the fortified dwelling of Sir Elidyr de Stackpole by John Campbell, ancestor of the Earls Cawdor, but demolished in 1962.

Follow the road from Stackpole to Freshwater East and proceed to Lamphey where the bishops of St David's built a stately palace. At the Dissolution of the Monasteries, the manor of Lamphey was granted to Richard Devereux whose grandson Robert, Earl of Essex and Queen Elizabeth's favourite, spent his childhood here.

Take the A4139 out of Lamphey to Hodgeston, where Thomas Young, Archbishop of York in the sixteenth century, was born, then on through Jameston to Manorbier. The entrance to Manorbier Castle is from the village, and beside it a road runs down to the beach.

From Manorbier follow the B4585 to rejoin the A4139 to Lydstep, beyond which is a splendid view of Caldey and St Margaret's Island. The road by-passes Penally and leads, over The Marshes, which used to be the tidal estuary of the Ritec, to Tenby which, as the leading resort in West Wales, has most of the things that the visitor may require.

Take the A478 out of Tenby and, beyond New Hedges, at SN 129033, turn right for Saundersfoot, which also caters for all the needs of tourist and holiday-maker.

The road out of Saundersfoot leaves the coast at Coppet Hall to encompass the grounds of Hean Castle and continues to Wiseman's Bridge. It then strays inland again as far as Summerhill (SN 153074) before descending to beach level at Amroth. The New Inn at Amroth marks the end of the journey, for the Pembrokeshire Coast National Park ends here, at the boundary of the former county of Pembroke.

Newport – Presely Hills – Cilgerran – Nevern

From Newport where there is a National Park Information Centre at Bank Cottage, Long Street, take the A487 to Cnwce (SN 049390), site of the gallows tree in feudal times, and bear left to follow the mountain road to the Gwaun Valley. Once out on the open mountain there are breathtaking views over Newport, the estuary of the Nevern, the sands and the bay, of Dinas Island and Fishguard Bay. Bedd Morus (SN 038365), 'the grave of Morris', a highwayman or a thwarted lover according to conflicting legends, is a standing stone probably of the Bronze Age; Sir Thomas Davies Lloyd, Lord of Cemais 1820–77, placed his initials upon it to mark the boundary between parishes.

The road makes hairpins before it arrives at the Dyffryn Arms (SN 026341) and crosses the Gwaun Valley road to Pont-faen church, where two stone pillars with inscribed crosses, of about the eighth century, stand in the churchyard.

Join the B4313 road from Fishguard at SN 014334 and follow to New Inn, and on towards Maenclochog, but do a dog-leg detour to Rosebush. The slate quarry was developed by Lord Macaulay's brother-in-law and his stepson; a railway from Clunderwen was completed in 1876, and extended to Fishguard in 1899, and an attempt was made to develop Rosebush as a popular mountain spa. Only faint traces of the laid-out gardens and lakes are to be seen, but the hotel, built of corrugated zinc, remains.

Maenclochog has a village green, with a church on a raised churchyard, inns and a general store. The name is made up of the Welsh *maen*, 'stone' or 'rock', and the Irish *cloch,* meaning the same.

Temple Druid, beyond Maenclochog, is said to have been built by Nash and appeared on the dust jacket of *The Happy Ending* which Leo Walmsley wrote when he lived there. At Llandeilo Isaf Farm at one time a skull reputed to be of St Teilo was kept: those who drank out of it were cured of a variety of ailments. Slates quarried at Llangolman roof the Palace of Westminster.

Gors Fawr, SN 135294, is the only stone circle in the Presely Hills: sixteen low pillars form the circle and there are two taller outliers to the north-east, in which direction roughly one sees the summit of Carn Menyn, the source of the bluestones of Stonehenge.

Mynachlogddu, 'the black monastery', was granted to the Benedictine Abbey at St Dogmael's. The Benedictines were known as the Black Monks. At Bethel chapel is the grave of Thomas Rees of Carnabwth, said to have been the leader when the Rebecca Riots broke out at Efailwen (SN 135353) on the night of 19 July 1839.

At SN 167334 turn right. The hill to the left is Foel Drygarn, 1,200ft (363m). The three cairns on its summit are Bronze Age burials, and there are the remains of a large Iron Age fort. Join the A478 and turn left for Crymych, a village that developed with the coming of the railway in 1875 and which continues as a busy agricultural centre; it has inns and shops.

Bear right at Crymych Arms along the A478 and beyond Blaenffos take the B4332 to Boncath, another railway village on the line to Cardigan, now closed.

The road passes the gates to Cilwendeg, a Georgian house that is now a home for the elderly, goes through Newchapel, and arrives at a junction at Penrhiw, Abercuch.

Here one has to make a choice: either turn right and follow the road to Cenarth to see the falls and, maybe, coracles on the Teifi, then turn left at Cenarth Bridge along the A484 to Llechryd; or else turn left, through the village of Abercuch, on to Manordeifi and along an old canal that served the tinplate works near Llechryd.

From Llechryd take the road running south; bear right at SN 217430 and right again at SN 209425 for Cilgerran, with castle, inns and shops.

Take the road leading west from Cilgerran to Pen-y-bryn and turn right along the A478 towards Cardigan. Turn sharp left at SN 180456 to join the A487 and at Croft bear right along the B4582 towards Nevern. At SN 125416 is a group of six Bronze Age barrows, known as Crugiau Cemais, and a splendid view towards the west.

Nevern is one of the jewels of the National Park and its church and churchyard should not be passed by without a visit.

Take the road out of Nevern, across the ancient bridge, to join the A487 at Temple Bar, and turn right for Newport.

The pink, round house, that looks like a piece of Staffordshire pottery, at SN 073392, was the lodge to Llwyngwair, now a country hotel.

The road to Newport has a fine view to its left of Carn Ingli, which has a large hill fort defended by massive walls between outcrops, and the remains of Iron Age huts and enclosures.

Fishguard – Presely Hills – Pentre Ifan – Gwaun Valley

From Fishguard take the A40 to Letterston and there turn left for Little Newcastle, or Casnewydd Bach, birthplace of Bartholomew Roberts the pirate. Born in 1682, he went to sea as a boy of thirteen. His ship was captured in 1718 by another Welsh pirate, Howel Davis. Davis was killed six weeks later and Roberts was elected by the crew to take his place. In a few years he took over 400 prizes. He was described as 'a tall, dark man, of good natural parts, and of reckless courage', and was said to have been comparatively humane and temperate, and a strict disciplinarian. He went into battle dressed flamboyantly in red damask, with a red feather in his hat, and proved an easy target when a man-o'-war came along. He was buried at sea on 5 February 1722.

Continue to Puncheston, named after Pontchardon in Normandy by an unknown Norman knight. Anglo-Norman place-names along the southern foothills of the Presely Hills mark the high tide of penetration from the south. The Welsh names survive however: this village was Casmael, the castle of Mael, before it was 'Pounchardon' as it appears in the thirteenth century. The Drovers' Arms is a reminder that the drovers passed here on their way to the Midlands.

On to Castlebythe, or Casfuwch, where there is a motte, and join the B4329 at Tufton Arms, so named after Caroline Tufton, daughter of the Earl of Thanet, who had married the local landowner. Turn left for New Inn and keep on climbing until Pen Bwlchgwynt, or Presely Top, is reached at SN 075323, at a height of 1,328ft (405m). Snowdonia may be seen from here on a clear day, and Dunkery Beacon, and sometimes the Wicklow Hills. A viewpoint, a little distance off the road to the left, on Foel Eryr, 1,535ft (468m), has a viewfinder that identifies landmarks in this splendid panorama.

Carry on downhill to Tafarnbwlch, formerly an inn, where the Ivorites met. Bear left and at SN 086344 pause to look across at the sweep of the Presely Hills.

At SN 088351 bear right and travel along a narrow road towards Pentre Ifan, one of the most impressive burial chambers in the country, which may be approached by stopping the car at SN 101370 and following a signposted path across a field.

Follow the road to SN 104379 and turn left; turn left again at SN 084385 and carry on to a T-junction at SN 074361; turn right and follow the road along the Gwaun Valley all the way back to Fishguard.

St David's – Treffgarne – Haverfordwest – Solva

From St David's, where there is a National Park Information Centre at the City Hall, take the A487 across open moorland to Croesgoch. Here there is an art gallery and Baptist Chapel with fine pointed windows. The Artramont Hotel takes its name from the Irish estate of a former local landowner.

At Mesur-y-dorth (SM 838307), 'the measure of the loaf', it is said pilgrims broke bread for the last time before reaching the shrine of the saint at St David's. A stone in the hedge bearing a ring-cross is of the eighth century. At SM 885318, below Mathry, bear right for Castle Morris, named after Maurice Fitzgerald, one of the Pembrokeshire knights who invaded Ireland in 1169.

Letterston takes its name from Letard Littleking, a Fleming, killed by the Welsh in 1137: he was described as 'the enemy of God and St David'.

At Letterston join the A40 and turn right. Wolfscastle has a motte and bailey, opposite the Wolfscastle Country Hotel. At Ford, near the Wolfe Inn, traces of a fortified Romano-British villa have been found.

The crags in the distance ahead are Maiden Castle and Poll Carn, rhyolitic lavas and tuffs of the Pre-Cambrian period.

Nant-y-Coy Mill (SM 956253) is now a craft shop. Above it are the Great Treffgarne Rocks, where there was an Iron Age fort and settlement. The road winds through the deep Treffgarne Gorge, cut by the Western Cleddau in glacial or post-glacial times.

The road passes Haverfordwest Aerodrome, which is the venue of the Pembrokeshire Agricultural Show each August. At the approach to Haverfordwest, on the right, is the Withybush Hospital and the Haverfordwest Rugby Club.

Haverfordwest has a National Park Information Centre at 40 High Street, and hotels, restaurants and car parks. It is the largest shopping centre in Pembrokeshire.

Follow the signs to St David's along the one-way street system and proceed along the A487. At SM 877205, Roch Castle stands out prominently to the right, and to the left there is a wide view of St Bride's Bay, with Grassholm a pimple on the horizon. Suddenly Newgale appears, with its storm beach, a great stretch of sand with ever-rolling breakers.

After climbing out of Newgale and passing Pencwm, Brawdy Airfield is on the right. To the left, below Pointz Castle Farm, the nightingale was last heard in Pembrokeshire.

Steep descent into Solva means a steep ascent the other side. Half-way up look over the wall to see if the tide is high.

Approaching St David's, note the monadnocks ahead, like Carn Llidi, 595ft (181m), and the absence of any indication of a cathedral.

Pembroke – Carew – Llawhaden – Narberth

From Pembroke where there is a National Park Information Centre at the Drill Hall, near the entrance to Pembroke Castle, take the A4075 until it joins the A477 and continue to the Carew turn at SN 047031. Carew Cheriton Church, with its high tower and corner steeple, has monuments to the Carew Family which are duplicated in Camerton Church, Somerset. Turn left along the A4075 for Carew Cross, opposite the Carew Inn: the inscription commemorates Maredudd son of Edwin, killed in 1035. Nearby is the entrance to Carew Castle.

At Whitehill, SN 055048, bear left and at SN 048067 turn right to Cresswell Quay which once exported coal from the nearby colliery. After crossing the Cresswell river, turn left for Lawrenny. Turn left in

Blackpool Mill, near Canaston Bridge (*Countryside Commission*)

the village for Lawrenny Quay, a popular yachting centre.

Return to Lawrenny and bear left to follow the minor road across Garron Pill to Landshipping, formerly a centre of coal mining, and coal exporting from Landshipping Quay; there is an inn and a pottery.

From Landshipping follow the road eastward and turn left at SN 042115 for Minwear Woods.

Blackpool Mill (SN 060144) was built in 1813 as a corn mill, with a horizontal millwheel, and continued to function until 1945. It is now a craft centre.

Where the road meets the A4075, turn left for Canaston Bridge; bear left on the A40 and then turn right for Llawhaden which has the fine ruins of a bishop's palace.

Leave Llawhaden by following the road towards the parish church and cross the Eastern Cleddau by Llawhaden Trout Farm. Bear right at SN 078173 and again at SN 094169; cross the A40 and continue to Narberth where there are inns and shops and the ruins of a castle. Join the A478 at Narberth and follow to Templeton where the Knights Templars had a hospice. The village is a street of farms, each with its own burgage.

Carry on along the A478 through Begelly and turn right at the roundabout to join the A477. Follow this through Broadmoor, Redberth and Sageston, and past the Carew turn to Milton. Bear right at Milton Brewery and at SN 020036 turn right for Upton Castle Grounds.

Return to SN 020036 and turn right for Cosheston, turn left in the village and continue till you meet the A4075 for Pembroke.

Scolton and Llys-y-frân Country Parks

From Haverfordwest, where there is a National Park Information Centre at 40 High Street, take the B4329 to Scolton (SM 991221) to visit the Country Park and Museum, which also has an arboretum and nature trail, open daily (except Mondays) from 1030 hours.

Scolton first appears in the records in 1326, among the vast possessions of Sir Guy de Brian, lord of Laugharne. In 1572 it was granted to Sir John Perrot and by 1600 it was in the possession of the Higgon family who remained there until 1974, when the estate was purchased by the Pembrokeshire County Council from Lieut-Colonel John Henry Victor Higgon OBE JP DL and converted to its present use. The Higgon family was prominent in the life of the county: four of its members were sheriffs, and the halberds carried by their liveried servants on such occasions may be seen in the entrance hall of the house. The house was burned down after being struck by lightning towards the end of the eighteenth century and was rebuilt for James Higgon to a design prepared by William Owen of Withybush at a cost of £3,000.

The stables and coach house, and a purpose-built exhibition hall, display collections of farm vehicles, machinery and equipment, craftsmen's tools and objects relating to various aspects of the past in Pembrokeshire. A saddle-tank locomotive, the *Margaret*, built in 1878 and used on the Maenclochog-Rosebush railway, is the central feature of a railway exhibit.

The country park consists of 40 acres (16ha) of landscaped parkland surrounded by woodland, with an arboretum, a pond, a butterfly garden and a nature trail. The Countryside Centre, which adjoins the house, contains interpretive displays.

To leave Scolton for Llys-y-frân, rejoin the B4329 for a short distance and turn right: proceed as far as SN 032220 and bear left for Llys-y-frân Reservoir.

Llys-y-frân Reservoir and Country Park (*B. R. Munt*)

Llys-y-frân Country Park (SN 040243) surrounds the reservoir that was built to impound and regulate the flow of the river Syfynwy so as to provide an adequate supply of water for the growing industrial and domestic demands of south Pembrokeshire. Work began on building the dam in 1968, after excavating the Ordovician slate which underlies the valley, and was completed three years later. The reservoir was opened by Princess Margaret on 9 May 1972.

Car parks and picnic areas are provided on both sides of the dam and there is a cafe open during the tourist season.

The reservoir is stocked with brown and rainbow trout. Fly-fishing, spinning and worm fishing are permitted, and fishing boats may be hired. Sailing dinghies may be launched from the main slipway, and canoes, sailboards and rowing boats are allowed on the western arm of the reservoir.

A nature trail sets off from the western car park, and there is a walk around the perimeter of the reservoir, which supports resident and migratory waterfowl.

11
EXPLORING THE TOWNS

The towns of Pembrokeshire are worth exploring. Haverfordwest, Tenby and Pembroke have castles and other evidences of their Norman origin, together with interesting churches, and unexpected nooks and corners. Milford (a new town in comparison) was built under an Act of Parliament of 1790, and became a leading British fishing port, then, more recently, the second oil port of Europe.

Haverfordwest

Start at the Old Bridge which, as a tablet commemorates, was built by 'the Good Sir John' Philipps of Picton Castle in 1726, and was crossed by King George IV on his way to Ireland in 1821. An earlier bridge, on or near this site, was crossed by Henry Tudor, on his march from Dale to Bosworth Field in 1485.

Past the Fishguard Arms is the Swan Square, where the Swan Hotel stood until it was demolished to make way for a store. Turn left into Bridge Street, the town's shopping centre. Narrow lanes lead to the new market and the riverside walk. The last, Friary Lane, led to the House of the Black Friars, or Dominicans, that was sited on the banks of the Western Cleddau.

From Castle Square, the town centre, cross to Quay Street, the haunt of sailors, and sometimes pirates, when Haverfordwest was one of the leading ports in Wales, trading from the Old Quay. The Bristol

Trader inn is a reminder of the days when a weekly packet and cargo vessels left here regularly for Bristol, and tied up at the Welsh Back there. The Wool Market recalls the time when Haverfordwest was the only staple town in Wales, and the warehouses along the quay were once full of corn and other produce awaiting shipment. The building at the far end was a Quaker Meeting House.

Return to Castle Square and walk up High Street, which has been described as 'perhaps the most beautiful street in Wales'. In its middle, opposite the Shire Hall, stood a row of houses, known as Short Row, until they were demolished early in the last century. The Shire Hall, with its classical façade, was built in 1835 on the site of the Quaker Meeting House: it was then that the Friends moved to the Old Quay.

The Pembrokeshire Coast National Park Information Centre is half-way up the street on the right.

Hill Lane, beside Munt's the Jewellers, climbs steeply to join Goat Street by Foley House. Cross Market Street to Hill Street. The Palace Cinema stands on the site of the Corn Market. Hill Street was the first street in Wales to have a flagstone pavement and was formerly known as King Street Flags. Albany Independent Chapel was built on the site of the Green Meeting, a private house used for worship by Dissenters from about 1638.

In 1758 at the Dragon Hotel, then a town house, was born the hero of Waterloo, General Sir Thomas Picton.

The wide open space of St Thomas's Green is transformed into a great colourful whirligig and charivari when the fair comes in May and October.

Return along Hill Street and turn into Horn's Lane opposite The Buttery. Go down a raised pavement towards the Library, a modern building, the round hall of which is much used for art exhibitions. A bronze plaque outside the library commemorates the last of fourteen visits to Pembrokeshire made by John Wesley in 1790 when he was in his eighty-eighth year.

St Mary's Church is one of the most impressive churches in the Principality. There are traces of a Norman foundation, but it was enlarged during the thirteenth century when the north aisle and the tower, which had a spire until it was taken down in 1801, were added. The arcade separating the north aisle from the nave has pointed arches with deep-cut mouldings springing from clustered pillars. These have interesting capitals, some of them amusing: a lamb biting the head of a serpent, an ape strumming a harp, a pig playing a *crwth* (type of fiddle), a monk with a turned-down tankard, and a woman showing her tongue to a leering grotesque. The fifteenth-century panelled oak roof of the nave springs from corbels of carved heads, male on the south and female on the north. A side-pew for the Mayor and the Sheriff has an elaborately carved bench-end portraying a knight slaying a dragon.

On the raised platform at the end of the nave is a font that may have been a holy-water stoup, a recess that may have been a confessional, and the effigy of a fifteenth-century pilgrim who, by the scallops on his scrip, had visited the shrine of St James at Compostela. Among the monuments in the church is a brass to the Mayor of 1642, a heart-rending epitaph to 'the lovely Hessy Jones', and memorials and hatchments of the Philipps family of Picton Castle, including 'the Good Sir John'.

Below the church is the building that once was known as the Town Assembly Rooms, sadly become ruinous. Here was the centre of social life throughout the winter season, where fashionable balls were held, attended by crinolined ladies conveyed in sedan chairs.

The Youth Centre, on Tower Hill, was formerly Tasker's School for Girls, named after Mary Tasker of Rudbaxton who in 1684 bequeathed her farm for the purpose of founding a charity school.

Mariners' Square is named after the Mariners' Inn, now the Hotel Mariners, the town's leading hotel. A print of 1797 shows a fox on the roof of the inn having escaped from a pack of hounds below.

Beyond the car park adjoining the Mariners is Spring Gardens; the upper houses have elaborate cast iron balconies and railings dating from the middle of the last century.

At the bottom of Barn Street there are three Nonconformist chapels in contrasting styles. Bethesda Baptist Chapel is 'Welsh Romanesque' built in 1878 by George Morgan of Carmarthen for £2,199. Tabernacle Congregational Chapel, 1874, was designed by Lawrence and Goodman in the Roman basilica style. The Wesleyan Chapel was erected in 1865 on the site of the Wesley Room, at the opening of which John Wesley had preached in 1772, but it is now closed and no longer a place of worship.

St Martin's Church was 'the castle church', built in Castleton, within the town walls, and it claims to be the oldest church in the town. It was rebuilt in the fourteenth century and restored in 1865. It has a stone spire and there is a priest's chamber over the door. The twelve stations of the cross are displayed and there is a modern crucifix hanging from the chancel arch.

The castle is open to the public and within its walls are the Castle Museum and Record Office. On leaving the castle, turn sharp left along Castle Back and walk down the steps to Castle Square and continue along Victoria Place, completed in 1839. Augustus John, though born in Tenby in 1878, spent his childhood years here, and it was here that his sister, Gwen John, was born.

The New Bridge was built in 1837, across the ford that had given Haverfordwest its name.

Tenby

From the Five Arches, which was the barbican of the South Gate, St George's Street leads to Tudor Square, so named after the prominent local family of Tudor. Tenby House, on the south side, was built for Sir William Paxton, a London banker who had made his fortune in India. He had rebuilt Middleton Hall in Carmarthenshire and built Paxton's Tower nearby to commemorate Nelson's victory at Trafalgar.

The Tudor Merchant's House on Quay Hill is basically fifteenth century. It is now the property of the National Trust and the Trust has an information office there. Plantagenet House, next door, is of the same period.

At the top of Bridge Street, opposite, lived the prolific artist, Charles Norris, who portrayed Georgian Tenby and left more than 1,200 drawings at his death in 1858. Norris was born at Hughenden Manor, near Beaconsfield, in 1779 and arrived in Tenby on board his yacht from Bristol in 1805. He had been attracted by the praises of his cousin Walter Savage Landor, the poet, who had fallen in love with the 'golden-haired Nancy Jones' at Tenby.

Bridge Street leads to Castle Square where Georgian houses, in varied pastel shades, look down upon the harbour. Here stood the Whitesand Gate guarding the access from the harbour to the town.

Tenby Museum and Art Gallery adjoins the castle grounds and has an exceptionally well arranged display of exhibits illustrating the past in the neighbourhood, and paintings by artists including Augustus and Gwen John.

The remains of Tenby Castle stand on Castle Hill. The marble statue is the Welsh national memorial to the Prince Consort, unveiled in 1865 by his son, the Duke of Connaught. The pieces of ordnance are remnants of the Civil Wars; other cannon serve as bollards on the quay.

Off Castle Beach is St Catherine's Rock surmounted by a nineteenth-century fort.

Beyond the Lifeboat House is Laston House, built in 1805 and rebuilt four years later after destruction by fire, as a sea-water bath house by Sir William Paxton. The adjacent Assembly Rooms were for the

Tenby Harbour, with Tenby Castle in the background (*Wales Tourist Board*)

quality and the cottages for the bath attendants.

In addition to providing a superior bath house, Sir William Paxton provided a theatre and other benefits for the town which made it attractive to visitors. They came by sea from Bristol and then by rail once the town had been connected to the main London line at Whitland in 1863. Bathing machines were installed, and bathers not wishing to use a machine had to appear 'in a proper costume' early in the morning or late at night. The resort became increasingly popular and people came to enjoy 'that peculiar hospitality which distinguishes the principality of Wales'.

A breakwater and quay were built in 1328, with a small chapel dedicated to St Julian, the patron saint of travellers, towards the end of the quay. Here fishermen prayed for a good harvest, and paid tithes of fish and oysters to the incumbent. In 1781, the chapel was converted into a bath house by Dr John Jones of Haverfordwest, and it was later used as a blacksmith's forge. It was demolished in 1842 and a new chapel, St Julian's Chapel, known as the Fishermen's Church, was erected on the beach in the harbour in 1878.

From Tenby harbour except on Saturdays and Sundays boats leave regularly for Caldey, and from Castle Beach when the tide is low.

From Castle Square, St Julian Street passes Lexden Terrace, built in 1843, with Ionic pilasters and plain recessed doorways. Turn left into Cob Lane which leads to the Paragon, passing Gunfort Gardens, where cannons were mounted when invasion was feared, and on to St Florence Parade through the Belmont Arch. The Arch was made in 1863 when the corporation gave consent to the Earl of Limerick to construct a carriageway to his new house, Belmont House, which is now part of the Imperial Hotel.

Along the Esplanade the Atlantic Hotel has a horse's head over the door and a tablet bearing the word 'Trayles'. This was the name of the horse that won the Ascot Gold Cup in 1889 for its owner Warren de la Rue, who came to live in Tenby in 1913 and built these premises. Further along is the Belgrave Hotel which Augustus John described in his autobiography, *Chiaroscuro,* as 'the big mauve house on the Esplanade in which I was born'.

St Florence Parade marches along with the town wall, passing a large square tower, and continues beyond the Five Arches as South Parade, which used to be known as The Whale or the Rope Walk. In 1784 the corporation gave Michael Morris a lease of the land for the purpose of establishing a rope walk at a rent of five shillings per annum.

The North Tower stands at the corner of White Lion Street and built into the angle of the wall is the De Valence Pavilion, named after William de Valence, Earl of Pembroke, who planned the town. It faces on to Upper Frog Street, formerly Frogmere, 'the pool of frogs'.

Where White Lion Street joins High Street stood the North Gate, demolished in 1782. The house next to the Royal Lion Hotel, with the Bath-stone facade, was a prize-winning design at the Great Exhibition of 1851.

The entrance to the Market Hall, in High Street, was built in 1829.

It has three limestone arches with cast-iron grilles, and a plaque above bearing the borough seal.

There was a row of houses between High Street and the churchyard, and among them was the house of Thomas White, who provided a ship for the young Henry Tudor to be taken for safety to Brittany in 1471.

St Mary's Church is one of the largest churches in Wales, probably built on the site of an earlier foundation that was destroyed during the sacking of the town by Llywelyn in 1260. In the fifteenth century, when Tenby flourished as a port, extensions were made that more than doubled the size of the church. The chancel was extended eastwards, and the wagon roof, set over its heightened walls, is the chief glory of the edifice. Among the monuments are the alabaster tombs of Thomas White and his son John; the painted wall monument of Thomas ap Rhys of Scotsborough and his family; and a tablet to the memory of Peggy Davies 'bathing woman 42 years to the ladies who visited Tenby' until she 'was seized with apoplexie and expired' in the water, at the age of eighty-two, in 1809. A plaque commemorates Robert Recorde, the sixteenth-century mathematician and scientist. Notable among the benefice holders were Giraldus Cambrensis (1210–23) and John Dee, the Queen's astrologer (1601–8).

In St George's Street, which leads back to the Five Arches, is the medieval Town Hall and, beneath it, was the town gaol.

Pembroke

The town of Pembroke lies along a narrow limestone ridge, with a street along its crest, extending from Eastgate to Westgate.

St Michael and All Angels' Church, near the Eastgate, was erected during the second half of the thirteenth century, but little remains of that edifice, which is shown by Speed and in a sketch by a French artist c1650 as having a central tower. The present church was built in 1887.

The street divides to form an island at one end of which is an impressive Wesleyan Chapel.

The building opposite the King's Arms has a clock tower which formerly had a cupola, and is decorated with leaden cherubs.

The Church of St Mary the Virgin was built during the thirteenth century, probably on an earlier site. On the north side of the chancel is a stone-carved panel on which is inscribed the name of William Adames, who died in 1607. There is also a monument, of about the same date, to Rowland Merike, a member of the Meyrick family of Bush. The church was restored in 1879.

A road beside the church runs down to Northgate, before crossing Pembroke Bridge, beside which stood the town mill.

A National Park Information Centre is situated at the Drill Hall, near the entrance to the castle.

From the old corbelled houses, across the road from the Barbican Gate, the springing of the arch of the Westgate may be traced. It is the only fragment left of the town's three gates.

Monkton Church stands on a part of the site of Monkton Priory. In 1098 Arnulf de Montgomery gave St Nicholas Church at Monkton, described as being 'within his castle of Pembroke', to the abbey of St Martin at Séez, in Normandy, along with twenty carucates of land, and, soon after, the Priory was founded. Much of its remains, including a dovecote, are incorporated in Priory Farm, but the choir and sanctuary form part of the present church.

The church, which was restored in 1887, has a long nave with Norman features and contains a number of monuments to the Owen family of Orielton and the Meyricks of Bush.

Monkton Old Hall nearby dates from the fifteenth century and was restored towards the end of the last century. It is a private residence.

Milford

Begin at The Rath, so named because it was mistakenly believed that the fort built here by the Royalists during the Civil War was a prehistoric *rath*, an Irish name used in mid-Pembrokeshire for an Iron Age hill fort. Above The Rath stood the beacon, or sailors' chapel, dedicated to St Thomas à Becket, which was a ruin until it was restored in 1935. There are seats in the well maintained public gardens, from which there is a panoramic view of the industrial development in Milford Haven.

Away to the left is the Gulf Oil Refinery; opposite is Texaco and alongside its jetty is that of the BP Oil Terminal now closed. Barely visible to the right is the jetty of the Esso Oil Refinery, closed in 1984, and beyond it is the Amoco jetty. The tall chimney stack to the left of Texaco belongs to the Pembroke Power Station. There is an open-air swimming pool below The Rath.

The Rath leads out along Sandhurst Road, which joins Hamilton Terrace beside St Katherine's Church. The Town Hall, on the left, is an imposing building erected in 1939 at a cost of £15,000. Apart from its municipal functions, it is used for art exhibitions and concerts, and is the centre of much of the town's social life. Next to it is the public library. In Mansfield Street, almost opposite, is a museum displaying features of the history of the town and of its fishing industry.

The dockyard, and the town, with its three parallel, terraced streets and intersecting side streets, were designed at the end of the eighteenth century by Jean-Louis Barailler, who had left Toulon during the French Revolution and had been appointed assistant to the Inspector-General of Naval Construction at the Admiralty. The three parallel streets, at first known as Front, Second and Third Streets, are now Hamilton Terrace, Charles Street and Robert Street, after Sir William Hamilton, Charles Greville and Robert Greville. Other streets bear the names of members of the Greville family: Greville, Fulke, Francis, Mansfield, Brooke and Warwick. The Quaker families are remembered in Starbuck Road, Nantucket Avenue and Dartmouth Gardens.

Near the end of Hamilton Terrace is the Lord Nelson Hotel. On 1 August 1800 Peter Cross announced that he was going to open the following month a 'spacious and elegant inn erected by Sir William Hamilton'. In 1802 Charles Greville had invited Lord Nelson and the Hamiltons to visit Milford and they arrived in time to celebrate the fourth anniversary of the Battle of the Nile, for which Greville had made elaborate arrangements. Nelson's praise of the dockyard and of the naval construction there, and his description of Milford Haven as one of the finest harbours he had ever seen, gave Greville the publicity he required for the success of the new town. The inn has been known, ever after, as the Lord Nelson Hotel.

Beneath Hamilton Terrace, the fish market extends for a ¼ mile (½km). In the 1920s Milford ranked fourth in importance to Hull, Grimsby and Fleetwood as a fishing port, with more than a hundred steam-trawlers landing over 40,000 tonnes a year. A record landing of 60,000 tonnes in 1946 was followed by a sharp decline in the industry.

Dartmouth Street leads off Hamilton Terrace. Along St Peter's Road to the left is the Torch Theatre and Youth Club.

In Dartmouth Gardens, off Dartmouth Street, is the Friends' Meeting House, built in 1811 on a site previously acquired as a burial ground by the Quakers when Abigail Starbuck died in 1801. The gravestones in the Quakers' Yard bear only the initials of those buried, and the date: for example, *SS 1803* and *AS 1801* on the graves of Samuel Starbuck and his wife Abigail.

Return along Dartmouth Street and follow Charles Street, the main shopping area, to Great North Road and turn right.

St Katherine's Church was consecrated in 1808. Charles Greville wished to place in the church the truck, or wooden disc, at the top of the mainmast of the French ship *L'Orient* as part of the baptismal font, to commemorate Nelson's visit to the town. The ship's captain, Louis Casabianca, had fought to the end at the battle of the Nile while his thirteen-year-old son 'stood on the burning deck'. However the Bishop of St David's objected to the presence of something that had 'been polluted by such a complication of blood and carnage as took place in the explosion of the *L'Orient*'. The truck was removed to the Royal United Services Institute in Whitehall. Nor would the bishop allow a porphyry urn, brought back from Egypt by the Bishop of Meath, to be used as a font, but the urn has remained as an ornament in the church.

Milford Haven, being a 'new' town established in 1790, cannot be expected to have any old buildings, but there are the remains of two, one unusual and the other, outside the town, ancient, which warrant a visit. These are the Observatory and Priory.

The Observatory may be reached following the road beyond Hamilton Terrace and crossing Victoria, or Hakin Bridge. This has a tablet commemorating the visit of George IV after his squadron had suffered a severe storm while returning from Ireland in September 1821. Then take St Lawrence Hill and at its junction with Waterloo Road turn right to Glebelands. The skeleton of the Observatory is all that remains of Charles Greville's proposal to establish 'The College of King George the Third . . . limited to Classes of Mathematicks and their Application to Mechanicks, Military and Naval and Civil Engineering, Construction of Ships, Navigation and Survey and drawing'. There is no evidence that the college ever functioned.

Pill Priory is at the top end of Hubberston Pill and may be reached by taking the Marble Hall Road, off Great North Road, and continuing along Cromwell Road. The naked chancel arch, which is most of what remains, stands spectacularly in the little village of Priory.

GAZETTEER

(Places marked * are discussed more fully elsewhere in the text.)

Abercastle/Abercastell (SM 853337)   A coastal hamlet, at the end of a drowned valley, from which schooners sailed carrying corn and other farm produce to the West Country and returned laden with merchandise that was sold at the local shop, aptly called the 'Bristol Trader'. Limestone brought from south Pembrokeshire was used to build a water mill, storehouses and a tavern, and to be burnt in limekilns, one of which survives, before being spread on the land.

Ynys y Castell may have been an early Christian site. Upon it is Bedd Bŷs Samson, 'the grave of Samson's finger', the finger with which he lifted the capstone on to the upright pillars of Carreg Samson, the chambered tomb at Longhouse farm above the bay. The tomb is an outstanding example of a passage-grave built by Neolithic people moving along this coast from about 2500BC.

A quiet little bay with a sandy beach, good for bathing and boating.

Abercuch (SN 248409)   A village in the vale of Cuch, where Pwyll, prince of Dyfed, according to *The Mabinogion,* chased away the hounds of the king of Annwn, the Celtic Hades, and set his own upon the stag they were following. For this he did heavy penance by having to change place with that monarch for a year and a day. Long the home of wood-turners who, until recent times, pursued their art in a manner almost unchanged since the Early Iron Age. In the garden of the Nag's Head inn the only coypu ever recorded in west Wales was killed in 1949.

Abereiddi (SM 796310)   A row of cottages, now much ruined, were the homes of industrious quarrymen who quarried slates that were taken by tramroad to Porth-gain on the other side of the headland known as Barry Island, whence St Barré, or Finbarr, is said to have sailed to his island retreat on Lake Gouganebarra in county Cork. A quarry hollowed in the dark slate cliffs was converted into an anchorage by local fishermen and is not inappropriately referred to as 'the Blue Lagoon'. The hair-pin graptolites *Didymograptus bifidus* are found in Ordovician

Cottage at Abereiddi, with grouted roof (B. R. *Munt*)

shales of the Llanvirn series; Llanvirn is a farmhouse above the bay. The little tower on Trwynycastell is a nineteenth-century navigation beacon.

The beach is ideal for family picnics.

Aber Mawr (SM 883347)   Isambard Kingdom Brunel once had the notion to develop this remote beach as a transatlantic port; traces of pier abutments and the bed of a railway line may still be seen. He changed his mind, however, and decided on Neyland instead. A submarine cable was laid from here to Ireland in 1883, and a telegraph station built, which has been converted into a private house.

Amroth (SN 170070)   Once a Norse settlement, called Earwere. A mound near the church is the site of a Norman castle where, it is said, the young prince Owain ap Cadwgan heard of the unrivalled beauty of Nest, the wife of Gerald de Windsor, and thereupon set off to abduct her. The present Amroth Castle was built around 1800, with a fine 'conservatory and grapery' attached to it. The church was enlarged in 1857 and restored in 1899: its tower has a projecting stair-turret and a prominent corbel-table. A rectangular building uncovered during the excavation of an earthwork at Trelissey farm is thought to have been a military outpost occupied from the second to the fourth centuries. Fossilised hazel nuts have been found among the tree stumps of the submerged forest, that sometimes appear at low tide, along with small flint arrowheads used by Mesolithic hunters.

Amroth is a popular holiday resort.

Angle (SM 865030)   The village's one street has colour-washed cottages and a colonnaded inn. A small fishermen's chapel in the churchyard was raised over a crypt in 1447 and has a stained-glass window showing Christ walking on the Sea of Galilee, and a priestly effigy. Tradition states that three co-heiresses built residences that remain as a pele-tower – a house with pointed stone windows – and The Hall. The village still retains a feudal shape.

West Angle Bay has a fine sandy beach. The nineteenth-century fort on Thorn Island has been converted into a small hotel.

Begelly (SN 118075) The name is a corruption of the Welsh *bugeildy*, 'shepherd's house', like Beguildy in Shropshire. The tall church tower commands a wide view over the surrounding countryside and was used as a watch tower even during the last war. A Norman castle mound was destroyed in 1941 so as to extend the churchyard. Augustus John spent some of his boyhood at the Big House and looked with envy upon the free-living gypsies on Kingsmoor Common below. The local collieries produced 50,000 tonnes of anthracite coal annually during the last century.

Boncath (SN 205384) A village that grew when the Whitland and Taf Vale Railway was extended to Cardigan in 1885. Ffynnone, nearby, was designed by John Nash in 1793 but the house was remodelled in 1904. Cilwendeg, now a home for the elderly, is a Georgian house, with a shell-lined grotto, that was built on the proceeds of the last privately owned lighthouse in Britain, the Skerries, off Anglesey. *Boncath* is the Welsh for 'buzzard'.

*Bosherston (SR 966948) At one time known as Stackpole Bosher, as distinct from Stackpole Elidyr, Bosherston is a kind of staging post for those who wish to gaze upon the beauty of the lily pools, and also for pilgrims to the cliff chapel of St Govan, but the parish church of St Michael should not be passed by. It has effigies of two fourteenth-century ladies and a churchyard cross of the same period bearing the head of Christ at its intersection.

NOTE *The area is closed during firing practice on Castlemartin ranges at times announced at Bosherston post office and in the local newspapers.*

*Broad Haven (SM 861135) As early as 1800 Broad Haven was a fashionable seaside resort, with bathing machines for those who were sufficiently intrepid to bathe in the sea. The wide stretch of sand is ideal for family outings, and the rollers provide excellent surf bathing.

The National Park Information Centre at Broad Haven specialises in marine life and, next to it, is a youth hostel with special facilities for the disabled. Adjoining both is a large National Park car park, with direct access to the beach.

Burton (SM 985054) The name indicates that Burton was 'a fortified settlement', and Burton Ferry was a small port on the Daugleddau: 'Le Gift of God of Burton' sailed from here in 1566. It is now popular as a centre for yachting and water-skiing. The Cleddau Bridge, begun in 1968, was not completed until seven years later. A section of the box girder construction collapsed in 1970 and work was suspended pending investigation into the type of structure. The cost of the bridge increased sixfold, which accounts for the high toll charges.

The parish church has a sixteenth-century altar tomb bearing the arms of the Wogan family of Boulston.

A burial chamber, known as the Hanging Stone, has a massive capstone supported on three pillars, and stands in a hedgerow between fields near the village, at SM 972082.

*Caldey (Ynys Pŷr) (SS 140965) During the summer season boats leave Tenby

The wide expanse of Broad Haven beach, off which is the Pembrokeshire Countryside Unit (*Wales Tourist Board*)

Harbour or Castle Beach regularly at low tide for the island of Caldey, landing at Priory Bay on a pier made of wartime concrete barges. At very low water passengers may be brought ashore on an ex-army amphibious landing craft.

A statue of St Samson, to whom the abbey and church are dedicated, stands near the perfumery in the 'village'. Nearby, St David's Church, the parish church, was also a refuge against raiders and pirates and at one time was used as a smithy.

The Abbey and its precincts may be visited by men only. The monks, who are of a reformed order of Cistercians, observe the Trappist vow of silence. They rise at three in the morning for vigils, attend lauds and concelebrated mass at six, terce at nine, sext at noon, nones at two, vespers at six and compline at half past seven, before retiring for the night. They partake of frustulum – a light breakfast – after mass, dinner after sext and a collation before compline.

The fuchsia hedges lead to the Old Priory and St Illtud's Church, which stands on the site of Pŷr's monastic settlement and of the priory that was subordinate to St Dogmael's. The buildings were neglected following the Dissolution of the monasteries and were used as farm buildings, a laundry and a malt house, until they were restored during the early part of the present century.

Beyond the Old Priory near the Abbey is the island farm, and a path continues to the Trinity House lighthouse, built in 1828 and now fully automatic. Here, at Chapel Point, is a wide view of the channel, with the Gower Peninsula to the east, Lundy Island ahead on the horizon and the great limestone cliffs of south Pembrokeshire to westward.

Camrose (SM 927202)   Camrose had a motte and bailey castle standing above the Camrose brook. At Wolfsdale the Bishop of St David's met Llywelyn the Great in 1217 and persuaded him from launching an attack on Haverfordwest, which he did three years later. James Berry, a farm servant at Wolfsdale, was the grandfather of Lord Buckland, Viscount Kemsley and Viscount Camrose. Keeston, originally Ketingston, and Tregetin in Welsh, has an earthwork consisting of three concentric lines of defence, and Walesland Rath was an oval enclosure with round huts of the third century BC.

*Carew/Caeriw (SN 048037)   Carew Castle is now leased to the National Park Authority, together with the French Mill, which was driven by water stored in the mill pond at full tide and is the only tidal mill in Wales that remains intact. Carew Cross is a memorial to Maredudd ab Edwin, killed in 1035. Carew Cheriton Church has tombs of the Carew family.

Castlemartin/Castell Martin (SR 915983)   Of the 'castle' there are only faint traces of ringwork and bailey, and no one knows who Martin was: the church is dedicated to St Michael. The organ in the church was built in 1842 and was brought from Sibton in Suffolk where it was played by Mendelssohn. The churchyard cross has been restored. The village pond has become a roundabout at the meeting of five roads, with seats and flower beds.

The Castlemartin Troop of the Pembroke Yeomanry Cavalry was raised by John Campbell of Stackpole, Lord Cawdor, and took an active part in repelling the French invaders at Fishguard in 1797, for which the regiment was allowed to wear 'Fishguard' on its standard and appointments. Castlemartin also gave its name to a breed of 'horned coal-black cattle', the Castlemartin Blacks, which were later merged with the Welsh Black Cattle.

*Cilgerran (SN 195430)   Cilgerran Castle, standing high above the Teifi Gorge, inspired the artist Richard Wilson, whose painting hangs in the National Museum of Wales, and J. M. W. Turner, whose work is at the Tate Gallery.

The church, except for its Norman tower, was restored so badly in 1839 that it had to be rased to the ground and rebuilt in 1855. Memorials are mostly to the Gower family; Admiral Sir Erasmus Gower was Governor of Newfoundland, 1804–07. A stone pillar in the churchyard is inscribed in Latin and in ogham with the name of Trenegussus, the son of Macutrenus, who lived, and died, in the sixth century.

Cilgerran was formerly a borough, with a portreeve, and a fair that was held on the feast of St Lawrence. The last beavers in Wales were recorded here in the twelfth century, and here also was 'the chiefest weir in Wales' where, it was claimed, a gross of salmon could be caught in a day. The gorge has been the haunt of coracle fishermen for centuries and is now the venue of the annual coracle regatta.

Crymych (SN 184339)   Standing where six roads meet, Crymych is the centre of a large agricultural area. Its growth as a village began when the Whitland and Taf Vale Railway arrived in 1875, on its way to Cardigan. The road from Cardigan to Tenby here crosses the prehistoric ridgeway that runs the length of the Presely Hills. Crymych lies between Moel Drygarn on the west and Y Freni Fawr on the east, and is a convenient place from which to tour the Presely Hills.

*Dale (SM 810058)   Dale appears first in the records as 'Villa de Vale'. The valley stretches from Dale to Westdale and is a continuation of the Ritec fault. Richard de Vale was lord of the manor of Dale in 1150; his descendant, Sir Robert de Vale, obtained a charter to hold a market and fair at Dale in 1293, and left only daughters, from whom were descended both Owain Glyn Dŵr and Henry Tudor. Henry returned to Dale in 1485 on his way to Bosworth.

Dale Castle is a private residence. The church has been restored beyond recognition.

Dale was a flourishing fishing village and port up to the early part of the last century, and it was also known for its brewed ale which sold well in Liverpool and Bristol. It is now one of the most popular sailing centres in west Wales, with a chandlery, an inn and a restaurant.

Dale Fort was built in 1856 as part of the first line of defence of the Milford Haven waterway, and is now a Field Studies Centre. Henry Tudor, when he landed at Mill Bay, is said to have built a chapel nearby, dedicated to St Ann; its site was used to build the St Ann's Head lighthouse.

Dinas Cross/Dinas (SN 011386)   Dinas, 'the little fort', is a long strung-out village that in part follows an ancient shore line. Roads lead off the A40 to Cwmyreglwys and Pwllgwaelod. At SN 012389 a road leads south over Dinas Mountain to Gwaun Valley.

Eglwyswrw (SN 142385)   Eglwyswrw was one of the twenty knights' fees (a division) of the barony of Cemais; its castle, a partial ringwork, is an overgrown mound. Its lord, in 1300, was David Martin, bishop of St David's, and he lived at the Court, a moated house. The Serjeant's Inn may be a reminder of the existence, across the road, of the armour house of the trained bands of the barony. The game of chess was played in the locality in pre-Norman times.

The 'church of St Wrw' stands in a circular churchyard, in a chantry chapel in which the saint was buried. Any corpse subsequently interred in the chapel was cast out, as the saint 'would not have any bedfellows'.

*Fishguard/Abergwaun (SM 958370)   The original settlement, Abergwaun, 'the estuary of the Gwaun', is now known as Lower Fishguard, or Cwm Abergwaun. It was a fishing port when the Norse visited these shores, for they called it Fishguard. In medieval times it was regarded as 'a fair haven and good harbour for barks and ships of small burthen' and, in addition to fish, quantities of grain and farm produce were exported. Before the end of the sixteenth century, however, the quay was 'in utter ruin and decay' and the inhabitants appealed to Queen Elizabeth, as lord of the manor of Fishguard, to cause it to be repaired.

The manor of Fishguard formed part of the barony of Cemais, the conqueror of which, Robert Fitzmartin, is said to have landed at Fishguard, and to have been greeted by the natives with a hail of boulders. Fishguard was one of the boroughs of the lordship, but it lost its charter during the Civil War and for a number of years was without a mayor.

The town was held to ransom by the privateer *Black Prince* in 1779, and bombarded when it refused to hand over the money. Fishguard Fort was built to ward off any recurrence but when invasion came, in 1797, the fort did not prove to be effective.

Richard Fenton the historian built a house, which he called Plas Glynamel, in the valley above Lower Fishguard. He was a friend of Garrick, Burke, Goldsmith and Joshua Reynolds, and author of *Historical Tour through Pembrokeshire*.

Goodwick/Wdig (SM 945382)   Goodwick was a fishing hamlet until about 1700, when William Rogers, a merchant of Minehead, acquired the house that

The entrance to Lower Fishguard, the best harbour in north Pembrokeshire (*Wales Tourist Board*)

stood above the little quay, and made his fortune by large-scale smuggling. The Fishguard Bay Hotel now stands on the site of the house.

When the railway came west, Isambard Brunel persuaded the South Wales Railway Company to make Fishguard, or more correctly Goodwick, its terminus, and also to construct a harbour from which packets could sail to Ireland. Work began on the line in 1847 but the project was abandoned when it was learned that the troubles in Ireland prevented the extension of the railway from Dublin and Cork to Waterford, and it was not until 1899 that work was resumed. The railway line reached Fishguard Harbour in 1906, and the cross-channel service to Ireland began, but attempts to establish a transatlantic port failed to succeed.

The battle of Pwll Wdig is said to have been fought on Goodwick Moor in 1074, when Trahaeaen, prince of Gwynedd, defeated Rhys ab Owen, prince of Deheubarth, and drove him like 'a frightened stag before the staghounds'.

Gumfreston (SN 109011)   It is difficult to believe that ships sailed out of Gumfreston up to the early part of the last century. This was until an embankment was built across the estuary of the Ritec so as to reclaim land from the sea but the result was marshes and sand dunes. The church, dedicated to St Lawrence, has traces of a fresco on the north wall of the nave depicting that saint's martyrdom. Scotsborough House, an utter ruin, was the home of the Perrots from 1300 and then, through marriage, of Thomas ap Rhys, whose painted tomb adorns St Mary's Church, Tenby. Daisyback Farm was the home of the ancestors of Benjamin Hall, later Lord Llanover, who gave his name to Big Ben. In 1607 a Tenby woman was charged with practising witchcraft at Gumfreston to the detriment of cattle and goods, but the sentence upon her is not known. One of the last duels fought in Wales took place on an April dawn in 1838 when two local magistrates drew pistols at the foot of Gumfreston Hill.

Gwaun Valley/Cwm Gwaun (SN 001352)   The loveliest of valleys, created by the rushing meltwater of the Ice Age glaciers, the Gwaun Valley stretches from Lower Fishguard to the Presely Hills. Some of its steep woodlands and wet valley floor are designated Sites of Special Scientific Interest. The Llannerch Alder Carr is a nature reserve. In and around the valley there have been no less than five churches. Llanllawer (SM 986360) has cross-incised stones and 'a sainted well' into which a bent pin could be dropped in order to wish ill to an adversary. Nearby, at Parc-y-Meirw, 'the field of the dead', is a rare alignment of eight pillar stones. Llanychaer church has been heavily renovated, and Llanychlwydog has been converted into a private residence. Pontfaen church has pillars inscribed with Latin crosses, and Cilgwyn (SN 077359) has a cross-incised stone built into the north-east exterior wall of the church. The people of the valley refused to recognise the change in the calendar in 1752 and consequently New Year's day continues to be celebrated on the thirteenth of January each year.

*Haverfordwest/Hwlffordd (SM 955155)   Haverfordwest emerges into history with the arrival of the Normans and the building of the castle on a prominent spur overlooking the Western Cleddau at its lowest fording place. The town grew in the shadow of the castle, and the original settlement, which included St Martin's Church, was known as Castleton, but the boundaries were extended during the thirteenth century so that the medieval town was of significant proportions and also a leading port.

Early in the twelfth century Haverfordwest received an infusion of Flemish immigrants who were given lands in mid-Pembrokeshire by Henry I. The town was captured by the Welsh under Gruffydd ap Rhys in 1136. In 1479 it received from Edward, Prince of Wales and Lord of Haverford, a charter decreeing that it should have a mayor who would also be a justice of the peace, coroner, clerk of the market and admiral of the port. In 1544 it became a county with its own sheriff, and in the following year was granted the right to have a Custos Rotulorum and to elect a Member of Parliament. It was given its own Lord Lieutenant in 1761.

The town's economic importance stemmed from its maritime trade, particularly with Bristol and Ireland. Vessels of some 200 tons (tonnes) could tie up at the quay, and barges could reach the Old Bridge. The port prospered until the railway came in 1853, although the little ships continued to arrive until well into the present century.

Haverfordwest was the county town of Pembrokeshire until the reorganisation of local government in 1974.

St Mary's Church is one of the finest churches in west Wales, but St Martin's is older. The town has a museum and a National Park Information Office, and is a good shopping centre.

Johnston (SM 932104)   Johnston, probably so named after its lord of the manor in the twelfth century, John de la Roche, is a busy village on the main road between Haverfordwest and Milford. David Lloyd George spent part of his early childhood at Bulford Farm. William James of Beacon Hill ran away to sea and became commander-in-chief of the marine forces of the East India Company. His capture of Severndroog brought him a baronetcy and a memorial, the Severndroog Tower, on top of Shooters Hill.

Kilgetty/Cilgeti (SN 126072)   Now a thriving agricultural centre, Kilgetty was formerly a settlement for coal miners working in the anthracite collieries in the surrounding area. Kilgetty House, with deer park, swans and statues, stood above

Stepaside and was the home of the Canon family until it passed by marriage to Sir Erasmus Philipps of Picton Castle. Sir Richard Philipps, born there in 1742, became the first Lord Milford.

On the edge of Kingsmoor Common, on the A477, the Kilgetty National Park and Wales Tourist Board Information Centre has an exhibition on the coal mining and ironstone working in the neighbourhood.

Lampeter Velfrey/Llanbedr Efelfre (SN 157145)   The name means 'the church of St Peter in Efelfre'. Efelfre, or Y Foelfre, was a district in the Welsh hundred of Cantref Gwarthaf and, later, in the lordship of Narberth. The parish church is dedicated either to Pedyr, a Welsh saint, or to the apostle Peter. It was restored in 1862 and has a number of memorials, including a Jacobean altar tomb in the Lady Chapel.

At one time it was said that the Ark came to rest at Blaengwaith Noah but the name is a corruption of Blaen Gwyddno, 'the source of the Gwyddno'. There is a promontory fort overlooking the Gwyddno valley, and a hill fort nearby at Castell Meherin.

Six roads meet at Tavernspite, where there was a hospice for pilgrims travelling to St David's. The Milford mail changed horses at the Plume of Feathers. Fulke Greville fought a duel here with John Jones of Ystrad, against whom he had lost the election of 1831.

Professor Glyn Daniel, the famous archaeologist, was born at Lampeter Velfrey.

*Lamphey/Llandyfái (SN 016005)   Lamphey was one of the manors of the Bishop of St David's and there was an episcopal residence here in the eleventh century. When Gerald de Windsor was besieged by the Welsh at Pembroke Castle in 1094 he sent a feigned letter to Arnulf de Montgomery stating that he had plenty of food. The letter was deliberately lost near the residence of Bishop Wilfred in the knowledge that he would convey its contents to the Welsh. Thus the siege was ended. Wilfred, having revealed his sympathy, was the last Welsh bishop to be appointed and was succeeded by the Norman, Bernard, in 1115.

The oldest surviving masonry at Lamphey Palace is a two-storey building dating from the early part of the thirteenth century. In the middle of the century the camera was added at the west end of the hall on the upper floor to serve as the bishop's private apartments. The Great Hall adjoining the south-east corner of the old hall was built by Bishop Gower (1328-47). He also added the arcaded parapet, as he had done at the Bishop's Palace at St David's, though it lacks the same fine detail and may have been the effort of local craftsmen.

On the great occasion of Sir Rhys ap Thomas's tournament at Carew Castle, the gallant company was entertained by Bishop Sherborne at Lamphey Palace.

In 1546 the manor of Lamphey was granted to Richard Devereux whose son was created Earl of Essex. Robert, the second Earl and Queen Elizabeth's favourite, spent his early days at Lamphey. Following his execution, the palace was allowed to fall into decay. In 1821 it was acquired by Charles Delamotte Mathias of Llangwarren, whose descendant placed it in the hands of the Commissioners of Works in 1925. Mathias built a handsome Georgian house in classical style, which is now a country hotel.

The parish church is dedicated to St Tyfai, a nephew of St Teilo.

Landshipping (SN 017113)   Although the origin of the name, 'long shippen', indicates an agricultural environment (shippen means cow house), Landshipping was a centre of the Daugleddau coalfield until the tide broke into the Garden Pit with the loss of over forty lives in 1844. A ruined house that once knew splendour, and derelict quays, are all that now remain, but there is a pottery and a welcome inn.

Lawrenny (SN 017069)   Lawrenny Quay, once a busy inland port, is now a popular sailing centre, with all the required facilities. The little village has a tall-towered church dedicated to St Caradog, above which is a picnic site offering wide views over the Carew and Cresswell rivers. Anthracite coal was exported from Cresswell Quay.

Little Haven (SM 857128)   At the foot of a steep hill in a narrow valley, and al-most Cornish, Little Haven is a much visited holiday and sailing centre, with a choice of popular inns. Settlands Bay has a sandy beach and may be approached at low tide. The view from The Point covers the half-moon of St Bride's Bay, from St David's Head to Skomer Island.

Little Newcastle/Cas Newydd Bach (SM 980290)   There is no trace of the castle as it was bull-dozed in the recent past by the local authority. It was a low motte, one of a line marking the northernmost intrusion of the Anglo-Normans up to the southern slopes of the Presely Hills. Bartholomew Roberts, the pirate, was born here in 1682.

Llanfyrnach (SN 220312)   St Brynach received a warm welcome here after fail-ing to find shelter elsewhere and gave the place his name. The church, along with eight others in north Pembrokeshire, is dedicated to him. Llanfyrnach was noted for its silver lead mine up to a century ago, which produced some 1,000 tons (tonnes) a year.

Llangwm (SM 990095)   Formerly famed for its oysters, Llangwm is now largely residential, although there is still fishing, some of it compass netting for salmon. This uses a net fixed to two poles which is lowered into the river on a rising tide and levered up smartly when the fisherman feels there is a fish in the net. The church is dedicated to St Jerome and has only a bellcote. It contains a canopied tomb with the effigy of a knight in armour, and another of a robed lady, probably members of the De la Roche family.

Benton Castle peeps over the trees above the well-wooded slopes of the banks of the Daugleddau.

Llanrhian (SM 819314)   The stepped gables and pitched roof of the tower of Llanrhian church give it the appearance of a stronghold. The rest was rebuilt in 1836, and restored extensively in 1891. Complaints about the dilapidation of the chancel were made in the early part of the fifteenth century. The church is dedi-cated to an unknown saint, Rhian or Rheian. The decagonal font has an inverted shield on each face, one of which bears a chevron between three ravens, the arms of Sir Rhys ap Thomas, whose descendant lived at nearby Rickeston. The road beside the church leads to Porth-gain.

Llanwnda (SM 933395)   Llanwnda Church serves the wide headland of Pen-caer, with its scattered farmsteads and cottages. It has a double bellcote and sanctus. There are five cross-incised stones built into the exterior wall of the church, one of which has a stylised human face. During the French invasion of 1797 a French officer stole the chalice and, when trying to sell it at Carmarthen, said he had brought it from France and that the inscription LANVNDA was a rendering of La Vendée. Below is the rugged coastline of Pen-caer, a peninsula having many prehistoric remains, including burial chambers at Garnwen, Pen-rhiw, Garnwnda and Garn Gyllwch, and an Iron Age hill fort on Garn Fawr. The French landed at Carreg Wastad on this coast.

Llawhaden/Llanhuadain (SN 070174)   The church, which stands on the banks of the Eastern Cleddau, is dedicated to St Aidan of Ferns, and the name of the village, Llanaiden, has been corrupted to Llawhaden. The castle, built by the bishops of St David's is entered from the village. A hospice for the use of wayfarers was built by Bishop Bek in 1287, but only a vaulted stone chamber remains. Ridgeway House, now a home for the elderly, was visited by Nelson in 1802, when it was the house of Admiral Sir Thomas Foley.

*Llys-y-frân (SN 040244)   The large reservoir at Llys-y-frân was opened by Princess Margaret in 1972 and parts of its surrounding land have been converted into a country park.

The little church has a medieval font with claws carved in the angles of the base. Its curate in 1741, the Rev Howel Davies, embraced Nonconformity and became known as 'the Apostle of Pembrokeshire'.

*Lydstep (SS 086983)   The ruin in the village is known as the Palace of Arms and is said to have been a hunting seat of the bishops of St David's. Lydstep Point is a National Trust property and has a nature trail.

Maenclochog (SN 083274)   A combined Welsh and Irish name: *maen* and *cloch* both mean 'rock', probably referring to Craig y Castell, 'the castle rock', which was the site of a small castle, all traces of which have vanished. It was captured by Llywelyn the Great in 1215 and by Llywelyn the Last in 1257. The church was rebuilt during the latter part of the last century, but the font is Norman. Two inscribed stones removed from nearby Llandeilo to the church are of particular interest in that they may commemorate two brothers: Coimagnus and Andagellus, the sons of Cavetus. The former has the inscription in Latin only, and the latter in Latin and ogham, and they date from the sixth century.

Manorbier/Maenor Bŷr (SS 066978)   The manor of Pŷr, whose island was Ynys Pŷr, or Caldey, and 'the paradise of all Wales' according to Giraldus Cambrensis, who was born in Manorbier Castle in 1146. The church of St James the Great, across the valley, has a Norman nave and tower; the chancel, transepts and aisles were added, or rebuilt, in the fourteenth century. The north transept has a window showing Master Richard, a monk, and Lady Margaret Beaufort, mother of Henry VII, together with the royal arms of King William II, and accommodates a tomb believed to be that of Sir John de Barri who granted the church to the priory at Monkton in 1301. East of the bay, on Priest's Nose, is a collapsed burial chamber, known as the King's Quoit. There is a sandy beach and dunes, between low red cliffs, and a convenient car park.

Marloes (SM 794085)   The most westerly village in south Pembrokeshire, Marloes has a clock tower, built in 1904 in memory of the fourth Lord Kensington, and a double-bellcote church which has a Norman font and a baptistry sunk in the floor. Marloes Mere was once famous for its leeches, which were much in demand in Harley Street. The lane behind the church leads to a National Park Authority car park from which there is a footpath to Marloes Sands. The main road continues through the village to Martin's Haven, boat stage to Skomer, and the Deer Park.

Mathry (SM 880320)   Mathry is a hill-top village with wide views over the surrounding countryside. Its circular churchyard may well have taken its shape from a
prehistoric site. The church is dedicated to the Seven Saints, septuplets saved
from being drowned by their impecunious father when St Teilo came upon the
scene and baptised them instead. An inscribed stone in the church porch commemorates Maccudicl the son of Caticus, who lived in the sixth century, and
there are two stones inscribed with crosses in the churchyard wall.

*Milford/Milffwrd (SM 905507)   Milford is a new town, born of an Act of
Parliament obtained by Sir William Hamilton in 1790 in order 'to make and
provide Quays, Docks, Piers and other erections and to establish a Market, with
proper Roads and Avenues thereto respectively within the Manor or Lordship of
Hubberston and Pill'. Sir William had obtained the manor by marriage to a local
heiress, Catherine Barlow, and it was after her death in 1782 that he conceived
the idea of building a town and harbour on the Haven. He was, by then, Envoy
Extraordinary to the Court at Naples and so he entrusted the task to his nephew
Charles Greville, son of the Earl of Warwick. Greville arranged for his mistress,
Emma Hart, to join Sir William at Naples and, in 1792, she became Lady
Hamilton.

Greville lost no time in providing harbour facilities and in 1793 he offered
favourable terms to a small group of Quaker whaling families from Dartmouth,
Nova Scotia, to establish a whaling station at Milford so as to provide spermaceti
oil to light the lamps of London. Seven families came but, with the invention of
coal-gas, there was no demand for the oil and the Quakers turned to trade and
business in the town. In 1796 Greville persuaded the Navy Board to build war-
ships in his dockyard and the keel of HMS *Milford,* of seventy-eight guns, was laid
that year.

Milford prospered for a while but, in 1814, the Admiralty moved the dockyard
to Paterchurch, which then became Pembroke Dock. Several attempts were made
to bring industry in its place and, in 1874, an Act of Parliament was obtained 'for
authorising the construction of Docks and other works upon or near Hubberston
Pill', but they were not open to receive shipping until 1888. Hopes for capturing
the transatlantic trade were dashed when the *City of Rome* called on her way from
New York to Liverpool and Mr Phineas Barnum and his menagerie had to be taken
off by tender some 6 miles (10km) from the docks.

The docks began to be used by fishing smacks and steam trawlers and Milford
quickly developed as a fishing port in the 1890s. By the 1920s it ranked fourth in
importance to Hull, Grimsby and Fleetwood, with over a hundred trawlers landing up to 47,000 tonnes a year. A record landing of close on 60,000 tonnes in 1946
was followed by a sharp decline in the industry. Just over a decade later, promise of
a new prosperity appeared with the obvious advantages of Milford Haven as a
potential oil port, able to accommodate large vessels of up to 56ft (17m) in
draught at all states of the tide.

Milford Haven/Aberdaugleddau   The Milford Haven waterway extends inland
into the heart of Pembrokeshire so that salt water flows beyond Haverfordwest on
the Western Cleddau and as far as Canaston Bridge on the Eastern Cleddau. The
pre-glacial valley was drowned with the melting of the ice following the last glacial
period, thus forming a *ria* that has provided one of the best natural harbours in the
world.

Promontory forts along the Haven bear witness to occupation during the Early Iron Age, and it is difficult to believe that ships of the Roman navy did not probe its waters. The Norsemen appear to have been regular visitors in their movements along the western seas and it is claimed that they may have wintered here, with a fleet of twenty-three ships, in 878. The name Milford derives from the Scandinavian meaning 'haven with sandy shores': the addition of Haven is therefore tautological. The Welsh name, which appears in *The Mabinogion*, is Aberdaugleddau, 'the estuary of the two Cleddau rivers'.

Although Milford Haven was described as 'the finest port in Christendom', little was done to provide it with defence against an enemy, except for a couple of blockhouses built for fear of the Spanish Armada. It was not until the middle of the last century that, in addition to the Defensible Barracks and the 'martello' towers at Pembroke Dock, the Government decided to establish forts on Stack Rock and Thorn Island, at Dale Point, South Hook, Hubberston, Popton Point and Chapel Bay, and inland at Scoveston.

The Esso Oil Refinery was opened in 1960 and in the following year the BP Ocean Terminal began to pump oil by pipeline to the Llandarcy Refinery near Swansea. There followed the Texaco Refinery in 1964; the Gulf Oil Refinery in 1968, and the Amoco Refinery in 1973. Milford Haven suddenly became Britain's leading oil port, with 10,000 ship movements conveying 60 million tonnes of cargo, mostly crude oil and petroleum products, in the peak year of 1974. The oil trade in the Haven has since declined: the Esso Refinery closed in 1984 and the BP Terminal in the following year.

Moylegrove/Trewyddel (SN 117447) This village of a few cottages and two chapels lies deep in a valley. Its name first appears as *grava Matildis*, the grove of Matilda, who was the wife of Robert Fitzmartin, the Norman invader of Cemais. The Welsh name may be interpreted as 'an Irishman's settlement'. There was a small harbour at Ceibwr where small coastal vessels brought cargoes of culm and limestone, and there was a little bootlegging at one time.

Mynachlogddu (SN 145305) The name means 'The black monastery', so called because its manor was granted by Robert Fitzmartin, lord of Cemais, to the Abbey of St Dogmael's, and the inhabitants of a part of St Dogmael's had a right of summer grazing for their cattle at Mynachlogddu. There is no evidence that there was a monastic settlement in the vicinity of this bleak moorland hamlet. Thomas Rees, otherwise Twm Carnabwth, leader of the first Rebecca Riot, lies buried at Bethel Chapel graveyard.

*Narberth/Arberth (SN 110146) The little town hall, *in medio strata* (in the middle of the street), displays the royal coat of arms. The bodega-like bonded stores of James Williams, brewers and wine merchants, look suitably Spanish. Otherwise Narberth is a typical small market town, serving a wide agricultural area.

The church, dedicated to St Andrew, has a thirteenth-century tower, but the rest was rebuilt in 1879 by Sir Thomas Jackson, who designed a front of Brasenose College, Oxford.

The Mabinogion, the earliest recorded Welsh tales, refer to Arberth as the chief court of Pwyll, prince of Dyfed, which has been identified as Sentence Castle, at Templeton, south of Narberth. Narberth Castle is on the south side of the town.

*Nevern/Nyfer (SN 083401) One of the prettiest hamlets in Wales, Nevern

Mounting block outside Nevern Church (B. R. *Munt*)

was once the stronghold of the ruler of the Welsh hundred of Cemais and, for a time, of the Norman lordship of Cemais following the occupation by Robert Fitzmartin in about 1100. The castle stands on a steep hill behind the church.

The church, with its squat tower, is almost hidden among ancient yew trees, one of which drips a blood-red sap. It is dedicated to its founder, St Brynach. St Brynach was an Irish missionary with a dozen dedications to his name covering an area that roughly coincides with the distribution of ogham-inscribed stones along ancient trackways and Roman roads. There are two fifth-century inscribed stones at Nevern: one, set in the windowsill in the north transept, is in memory of Maglocunus the son of Clutorius, whose name is written both in Latin and in ogham; the other, standing by the church porch, bears the name of Vitalianus, described as *emeritus*, and is also bilingual. The high cross, with its fretted and interlaced panels and indecipherable inscriptions, is of the eleventh century. Apart from the Norman tower, the church is late Perpendicular, but it was completely renovated in 1864.

*Newport/Trefdraeth (SN 057392)   The earliest evidence of human habitation in north Pembrokeshire is found at a Mesolithic site at Newport Bridge, and there is a Neolithic burial chamber, Carreg Goetan Arthur, nearby, while above the town is the great Iron Age fort of Carn Ingli. The original Welsh name Trefdraeth, 'the town on the shore', suggests a pre-Norman settlement on the estuary.

The town of Newport grew in the shadow of the castle and became the *caput* (capital) of the barony of Cemais. It received its first charter some time before 1215 and was granted a Mayor 'in consultation with the lord' of the barony. The mayor is still appointed in this unique manner and he presides over the Court Baron and Court Leet (local courts).

St Mary's Church has a thirteenth-century tower with stepped buttresses. It was enlarged in 1835 and again restored in 1879. The font is Norman and cushion-type, and there is a fourteenth-century coffin slab inscribed in memory of an unknown person 'who lies here: may God have mercy on his soul'. Near the west door, in the churchyard, is an early Christian monument bearing a ring cross. The church chapel, built in 1799 by early Methodists wishing to have the sacrament administered by their own ministers, has the original furniture.

Newport was a busy port throughout the centuries and little ships came in on the tide bearing cargoes of coal until 1934.

*Neyland (SM 965051) The creation of Isambard Kingdom Brunel after he had abandoned the idea of making Fishguard a great port, Neyland became the terminus for the South Wales Railway in 1856. Hitherto, it had been a small fishing village. Brunel also planned to capture the transatlantic trade, and brought his *Great Eastern,* then the largest vessel ever built, to lie up in the Haven at Neyland. When the railway came to Milford in 1863, Neyland lost its place as the only terminus, and the Irish traffic went to Fishguard, after all, from 1906. It remained as a railway depot until 1955, and the car ferry sailed from here to Hobbs Point until the Cleddau Bridge was completed in 1975.

*Pembroke/Penfro (SM 983015) Pembroke derives its name from the Welsh *pen* (end) and *bro* (land), 'land's end'. Although Roman coins have been found during restoration work on the castle, there is no evidence to suggest that the narrow peninsula on which the town stands was occupied before the arrival of the Normans.

Pembroke's prosperity during the medieval period began to wane when it ceased to be the *caput* of an earldom, under the Act of Union of 1536, and Haverfordwest took its place as the county town. It continued as a busy market town, and a centre for tourists visiting one of the most important and impressive castles in the country.

*Pembroke Dock/Doc Penfro (SM 966034) After the Admiralty had removed the naval dockyard from Milford across the Haven to Paterchurch in 1814, a new town was built on a gridiron plan, with wide streets. An obelisk on Albion Square records that 'the town was built almost entirely by the working classes who by their thrift and industry erected during the century upwards of 2,000 houses'. It became known as Pembroke Dock. In 1816 the first ships, the *Valorous* and the *Ariadne,* were launched. By the time the dockyard closed in 1926, more than 250 ships had been built, including the first steam man-o'-war, the first propeller-driven warship, and the first of many royal yachts, the *Victoria and Albert.*

The martello towers at either end of the dockyard were built in 1857 as part of the Haven's defence system. (They are not real martello towers, but are known as such). The Defensible Barracks on Barrack Hill had been erected twelve years earlier to accommodate a garrison of 500.

In 1930 Pembroke Dock became a seaplane station for the Royal Air Force and, later, a base for Sunderland flying-boats of Coastal Command. During the war it suffered heavily from enemy aircraft.

Penally/Penalun (SS 118991) The parish church of Penally contains an eleventh century wheel-head cross, of the same type as the high crosses at Nevern and Carew, and the broken shafts of another two. There is an early Christian connection as this would appear to have been a landing place for the Celtic saints on their way, following the trans-peninsular route, to St David's and on to Ireland. In the vicinity, in the sixth century, was born St Teilo, the founder of Llandaff Cathedral, whose great monastery was at Llandeilo, on the river Towy. In the church are the thirteenth-century tombs of William de Naunton and his wife Ismay.

Porth-gain (SM 814327) Porth-gain has an air of dereliction due to the exploitation of its geological resources during the latter half of the last century. Slate quarried at Abereiddi was brought here along a tramroad for export, and a railway tunnel was cut so as to bring clay for the manufacture of bricks, and high-quality granite, for which Porth-gain became best known. The stone was used for the erection of public buildings in London, Liverpool and Dublin, and was also crushed and graded and stored in hoppers ready for shipping to distant parts of the country for the metalling of roads. The Porth-gain Village Industries Limited was established in 1878 and continued to flourish until the early part of this century, but it ceased operations in 1931 and for the next fifty years Porth-gain was a scene of desolation, save for the activities of the local fishermen. In 1983 the National Park Authority acquired the harbour and the industrial remains and, in the process, assisted the villagers to purchase their homes. The grouted roofs of the row of cottages, known as The Street, were replaced by Caernarfon slates salvaged from a vessel that sank off Ramsey many years ago.

Pwllcrochan (SM 922027)　Pwllcrochan, 'cauldron pool', is one of a number of place-names that has remained Welsh in an area that has been anglicised for 900 years. In the north transeptal chapel an inscribed stone records the erection of the parish church by Ralph Beneger in 1342. There was a clash of arms in the churchyard between invading Royalists and Parliament forces during the Civil War.

Rhoscrowther (SM 904022)　The Norman church, dedicated to St Decumanus, was restored early this century. Above the porch, with its cobbled floor, is a figure depicting the risen Christ seated on a tomb with pierced hands raised. In the south transept is the recumbent effigy of a fourteenth-century lady.

Eastington was a fortified house with a low squat tower and a plain vaulted undercroft, dating from the fifteenth century.

*Roch/Y Garn (SM 881212)　Adam de la Roche, fearing that he would die of the bite of a serpent, built a castle upon a crag beyond the reach of any reptile, but when a servant brought in some firewood, a viper wriggled out and Adam was doomed.

The parish church, which stands within a raised circular churchyard, was rebuilt except for the porch in 1860.

Rosebush (SN 074293)　A slate quarry on the slopes of the Presely Hills was purchased by Edward Cropper, Member of Parliament for Penshurst, who built a row of cottages to accommodate the quarrymen, and a small hotel of corrugated iron. Rosebush was connected by railway to Clunderwen and Fishguard. Cropper died in 1877 and it was left to his stepson, John Babington Macaulay, a nephew of Lord Macaulay, to develop Rosebush as a mountain holiday resort, but without success. The quarries closed in 1906 but the railway remained in use until 1949.

Rosebush reservoir is popular with anglers.

Rosemarket (SM 953084)　'The market in Rhos', one of the hundreds (divisions) of Dyfed was granted to the Knights Hospitallers of Slebech in the twelfth century. Rosemarket claims to be the birthplace of Lucy Walter, mistress of Charles II and mother of the Duke of Monmouth, and it is certain that Anna Williams was born here. She was a figure in London literary circles and when she became blind was befriended by Dr Samuel Johnson.

Rudbaxton (SM 961204)　In the parish church dedicated to St Michael is a colourful monument with almost life-size figures, most of them carrying human skulls, raised in memory of members of the Howard family of Flether Hill. A bust commemorates General Sir Thomas Picton, whose family home was at nearby Poyston. After his heroic death at Waterloo, his body was interred at St George's churchyard, Hanover Square, and was later removed to St Paul's Cathedral. A brass plate remembers William Laud who held the living of Rudbaxton when Bishop of St David's; he later became Archbishop of Canterbury and was beheaded for treason in 1645.

St Bride's (SM 803109)   The Irish saint, Bride, or Brigit, may be identified with the Celtic fertility goddess Brigantia, to whom women made offerings at wells so that they might bear children. With the coming of Christianity she became sanctified and was nominated as the midwife of the Virgin Mary.

St Bride of Kildare has more dedications in Wales than all the other Irish saints together although she never left her native shores. They were probably brought by Irish colonisers in the sixth and seventh centuries.

The chapel dedicated to her at St Bride's Haven was converted into a herring salting house by the local fishermen and, in accordance with a local prophecy, it was swept away by the sea.

*St David's/Tyddewi (SM 753253)   'And so we came to the end of the world where the Patron Saint of Wales sleeps by the western sea': thus Francis Kilvert spoke for all pilgrims to the shrine of St David.

St David's lies to the east and south of the Cathedral Close which was a separate parish before the reorganisation of local government. It was a borough, with a mayor appointed annually up to 1925 by the steward of the bishop. The first sign of antiquity is the medieval cross standing on a sloping square, immediately before one obtains an eye-level view of the pinnacles of the Cathedral tower.

The National Park Information Centre is at the City Hall in High Street.

*St Dogmael's/Llandudoch (SN 165460)   The fishermen cast their seine nets, in a manner unchanged for centuries, during the salmon season at St Dogmael's, and a tradition of blessing the nets has been revived.

Robert Fitzmartin, lord of Cemais, brought monks of the Reformed Benedictine Order from the Abbey of Tiron, near Chartres, to St Dogmael's, in 1115, to found a priory that was soon raised to the status of an abbey and endowed with lands and with the subordinate priories of Caldey and Pill, and Glascarreg in county Wexford. The ruins are well preserved and are much as they appear in the Buck's engraving of 1740.

The abbey was built on, or near, the site of the ancient monastery of Llandudoch that was ravaged by the Vikings in 987. Early Christian monuments, placed within the Abbey grounds in 1847 but now in the parish church, include a sixth-century pillar inscribed in Latin and ogham with the name of Sagranus the son of Cunotamus.

The mill pond opposite the entrance to the Abbey stores water to drive the restored mill wheel at Y Felin, producing stoneground wholemeal flour.

The port of St Dogmael's once had a fleet of forty fishing vessels, and conducted a regular coastal trade. It is now a popular sailing centre, and there are boat trips to Cemais Head and around Cardigan Island, which is a nature reserve owned by the West Wales Trust for Nature Conservation and carries a flock of Soay sheep.

Poppit Sands has a fine sandy beach, with car park and facilities.

St Florence (SN 082013)   A village of farmsteads and cottages gathered around the tall-towered Norman church dedicated to St Florentius. The church has a brass plate commemorating Robert Rudd, Archdeacon of St David's, imprisoned by Cromwell. In the village there are examples of the typical solid round chimneys, and traces of the wall that encircled a deer park. Until the Ritec estuary was dammed in 1820 the sea reached St Florence.

The Manor House Wildlife Park has animal and bird enclosures, an aquarium and a reptile house.

St Ishmael's (SM 834073)   There is no trace of the monastery of St Ishmael, but the inlet below the bellcote church is still known as Monk Haven. The church stands in a profusion of trees and shrubs in a green valley and probably occupies the site of an earlier foundation, as indicated by the cross-incised stones near the Norman font. A broken, floriated cross is fourteenth century. In 1306 when the church was annexed to the Priory of St Peter at Gloucester, the prior appointed to the living a young person 'being under age and in tutelage', who died while still a minor.

St Ishmael's Tump, rising some 15ft (4½m) from a ditch in a field north of the village, is a fine example of a Norman motte.

*Saundersfoot (SN 137048)   A harbour was built at Saundersfoot in 1829 for the export of anthracite coal mined in the surrounding collieries, and the pig iron produced at the Stepaside Ironworks from 1849 onward. Horse-drawn trams carried the coal and iron on a tramway that travelled along The Strand, until a locomotive was purchased in 1915. The iron furnaces closed in 1877 but the coal mines continued to produce coal until the outbreak of the last war.

Today the harbour is alive with sailing boats and other pleasure craft, and Saundersfoot is one of the leading holiday resorts of west Wales.

The parish church of St Issell's, which lies in a sylvan setting outside the village, is mid-thirteenth century but greatly restored.

Hean Castle was built in 1876 by Charles Vickerman, who had acquired the collieries and the harbour. In 1899 it was purchased by the first Lord Merthyr, whose descendant resides there.

*Solva/Solfach (SM 805245)   A curved creek and steep slopes hung with gorse provide the setting for the pretty village of Solva. Tall-masted pleasure boats muster in the little harbour, where a fleet of coasters formerly anchored. Warehouses were built to meet the demands of the sea trade.

In 1775 a wooden lighthouse was assembled at Solva and erected on the dangerous reef of The Smalls. When it proved unsatisfactory, a more solid structure was built there, of granite brought from Bodmin and trimmed at Solva before being shipped out from Trinity Quay.

The Gribin, across the inlet, is a narrow ridge of headland, on top of which is an Early Iron Age fort, and beyond which is Gwadn beach.

Lower Solva's one street has shops, inns, a National Trust shop, and, in a converted chapel, a Nectarium teeming with tropical butterflies.

Tenby/Dinbych-y-Pysgod (SN 132004)   A poem of the ninth century, 'In Praise of Tenby', speaks of the hospitality the poet had received at the hands of Bleiddudd, lord of 'the fine fortress that stands above the sea' at Dinbych (the little fort), of which 'Tenby' is an anglicisation. It later became known as Dinbych-y-Pysgod (the little fort of the fishes) to distinguish it from the other Dinbych (Denbigh) in north Wales.

Little is known of the early history of Tenby, although there are evidences of early settlement in the vicinity, from the Old Stone Age occupation of caves at Hoyle's Mouth and Longbury Bank in the Ritec valley, and on Caldey.

The Normans came and built a castle which was captured by the sons of Gruffydd ap Rhys in 1153, who slew its garrison. The town was laid waste by the Welsh in 1187, and again in 1260 by Llywelyn the Last, who also destroyed the castle. A new walled town was planned by William de Valence, Earl of Pembroke, and the street pattern probably dates from that period. The walls were strengthened in 1457 by order of Jasper Tudor, Earl of Pembroke, who made them over to the mayor and burgesses, and repaired during the Armada scare in 1588. The South Gate barbican had two arches, which have portcullis slots, and three more apertures were made, by order of the Tenby Corporation, in the nineteenth century: hence 'Five Arches'. The Corporation proposed to demolish the barbican in 1873, so as to improve the flow of traffic, but an Order in Chancery was obtained by a Tenby physician, as recorded on a tablet on the wall. The North Gate, set across High Street at its junction with White Lion Street, and the Whitesand and Quay Gates, were destroyed.

At the beginning of the Civil Wars, Tenby was held for Parliament but surrendered to the Royalists a year later, only to be recaptured within months by the Roundheads. In 1648, the people of Tenby rallied to the cause of John Poyer, mayor of Pembroke, who had turned against Parliament, and Cromwell, who was at Pembroke, sent a force to besiege the town, which had to yield after two weeks.

Tenby was busy as a port during the Middle Ages, trading with France, Spain and Portugal, and particularly with ports along the Bristol Channel. Tenby merchants were exempted dues at the port of Bristol from 1423. Trade declined, however, and by the end of the eighteenth century Tenby was described as 'the most complete ruins of an old town', but it was not long before it began to develop as a holiday resort.

There is a National Park Information Centre at The Norton.

Trefin (SM 840325) A mock mayor used to be installed each year on a 'chair' of natural rock in the village of Trefin, but at one time it had a real mayor and a court leet. A fair also used to be held on the feast of St Martin at which traditional pies, known as *pasteiod Ffair Fartin,* were sold.

The ruined mill at Aberfelin (SM 834327) inspired the Welsh poet, Crwys, to write *Melin Trefin,* 'the mill at Trefin', one of the best loved lyrics in the Welsh language.

Wiston/Cas-wis (SN 022180) Wiston takes the name of its founder, Wizo, a Flemish immigrant who was granted the lordship of Daugleddau by Henry I and built a castle here. A mass of bones found while renovating the church in 1864 were believed to be the remains of those slain nearby in 1645 at the battle of Colby Moor when the Royalists lost 150 men.

WELSH PLACE-NAMES

The visitor to Wales often gets tongue-tied at attempts to pronounce Welsh place-names. This is understandable as the value of a number of the letters in the Welsh alphabet differs from that in English, and it may be helpful if a short explanation of these were given.

Welsh pronouncing is phonetic and robust, and each letter is given its full value. The alphabet has no *j*, *k*, *q*, *v*, *x* or *z*, but it has *ch*, *dd*, *ff* and *ll* as additional consonants.

The vowels may be short or long, only sometimes indicated by a circumflex. The letters *w* and *y* are also vowels in Welsh. Vowels are short when followed by *c*, *m*, *ng*, *p*, *t*, or by two or more consonants, and long when followed by *b*, *ch*, *d*, *f*, *ff*, *g*, *s*, *th*. The sound values of the vowels are approximately as follows:

Long	Short
a as in *barn*	*a* as in *ban*
e as in *pane*	*e* as in *pen*
i as in *eel*	*i* as in *ill*
o as in *dole*	*o* as in *doll*
u as in *keel*	*u* as in *kill*
w as in *pool*	*w* as in *pull*
y as in *fur*	*y* as in *fun*
or as in *dean*	or as in *din*

The consonants *b*, *d*, *h*, *l*, *m*, *n*, *p*, *t* have the same sound as they have in English. As for the others:

c is always hard, as in *cat*
ch guttural, as in *loch*
dd soft, as in *thou*
f is pronounced *v*
ff like *f* in *friendly*

g is hard, as in *go*
r is trilled, as in *merry*
s is hard, as in *essay*
ll is nothing like *kl* or *thl* but is produced, with a little practice, by placing the tongue against the roof of the mouth and hissing like an angry gander.

The following have their own distinctive sounds:
ng as in *long,* and sometimes as *longer,* as in *Bangor*
ph as in *pheasant*
rh as in *rhinoceros*
th as in *plethora.*

The mutation of initial consonants sometimes presents difficulties, particularly when searching for a word in the Welsh dictionary. The consonants *p, t, c, b, d, g, m, ll,* and *rh* soften to *b, d, g, f, dd,* (*g* disappears), *f, l,* and *r* respectively in circumstances such as:

(a) when a noun follows the preposition *ar* (upon); *ar* + *perth* becomes Arberth; *ar* + *coed,* Argoed
(b) when a feminine noun follows the definite article; *y* + *pont* becomes Y Bont; *y* + *magwyr,* Y Fagwyr
(c) when an adjective follows a feminine noun: *Ffynnon* + *glas* becomes Ffynnon-las; *croes* + *coch,* Croesgoch
(d) when the genitive follows a feminine noun: *tref* + *traeth* gives Trefdraeth
(e) when a personal name in the genitive follows a masculine noun: *ty* + *Dewi* becomes Tyddewi
(f) when a noun or adjective is the second element in a compound: *gwyn* + *bryn* becomes Gwynfryn; *efail* + *bach,* Efailfach
(g) when a noun follows an adjective: *hen* + *tre* becomes Hendre, except in the case of *ll*: *hen* + *llan* remains Henllan.

Welsh place-names appear mostly, as may be expected, in the Welsh area that lies to the north of a line stretching from Newgale through Treffgarne, but many survive in Little England beyond Wales to the south of that line, though often in a form that is not easily recognisable. Hentland, Trefloyne and Crunwere do not vary much from Henllan, Trellwyn and Cronwern, but it is not so apparent that Llawhaden, Begelly and Tenby derive from Llan Aidan, Bugeildy and Dinbych. Some, like Llangwm, Narberth, Pwllcrochan and Rhoscrowther have remained with little or no corruption.

In the Welshery of the north, a number of places retain their original English names, given to them at the time of the Norman occupation. Such are the small garrison town of Newport, the manors of Moylegrove and Monington, and the villages that mark the northernmost penetration from the south, like Little Newcastle, Puncheston, New Moat and Henry's Moat.

The Welsh place-names are often descriptive of location, as Penfro (land's end), Trefdraeth (town on the shore) or of physical features, as Sychbant (dry valley), Pencnwc (top of a knoll). They sometimes bear the names of persons, otherwise forgotten, as at Carn Ingli and Castell Martin, and of saints, some known, like Llandeilo and Llanfrynach, and others but a name, as in Llanhywel and Eglwyswrw.

The following list may be of help in understanding the meaning of Welsh place-names.

Welsh word	*English meaning*	*Example of place-name*
aber	estuary, confluence	Abereiddi
afanc	beaver, monster	Beddyrafanc
afon	river	Afon Alun
allt	wood, hill, slope	Penrallt
ar	upon	Arberth
atsol	fallow	Atsol-wen
bach	little	Casnewydd-bach
bachell	corner	Fachelich
bâl	summit	Pen-y-bâl
banadl	broom (the plant)	Llainbanadl
banc	bank, slope	Pen-y-banc
barcut, barcutan	kite	Stacan Barcutan
bedd	grave	Bedd Morus
bedw	birch	Llanfihangel-Penbedw
beri	kite	Penberi
betws	chapel of ease	Betws
blaen	source, head, end	Blaenffos
blaidd	wolf	Casblaidd
boncath	buzzard	Boncath
bont *see* pont		
breni	front, rim, prow	Y Freni Fawr
bro	region, country	Penfro
bron	breast (of hill)	Fron-las
brwyn	rushes	Brwynant
bryn	hill	Brynberian
bugail	shepherd	Begelly
bwch	buck	Penbwchdy
bwlch	pass	Bwlch-y-groes
caer(au)	fort(s)	Caerau Gaer
cam	crooked, bent	Y Gamlyn
canol	middle	Felinganol
capel	chapel	Capel Colman
carn	cairn, outcrop	Carn Llidi
carnedd	cairn, tumulus	Carnedd Meibion Owen
carreg	stone, rock	Carreg Edrywy
cas	castle	Casmael
castell	castle, stronghold	Castell Martin
cawsai	causeway	Pengawsai
cefn	ridge	Cefn-y-dre
cegin	ridge	Pengegin
celyn	holly	Llwyncelyn
celli	grove, copse	Y Gelli
cemais	bends, bays	Pen Cemais
ceunant	ravine, brook	Ceunant
cigfran	raven	Felin-gigfran
cil	corner, retreat	Cilgerran
cilfach	cove, creek, nook	Gilfach

Welsh word	English meaning	Example of place-name
clastir	glebeland	Clastir
clawdd	hedge, dyke	Clawdd-cam
cleddau	sword	Afon Cleddau
clegyr	rock, cairn	Clegyr Boia
cloch	crag, rock	Maenclochog
clôg	cliff, rock	Y Glôg
clun	meadow	Clunderwen
clydach	torrent	Pont Clydach
cnwc	hillock, knoll	Pencnwc
coch	red	Fagwyr-goch
coed	trees, wood	Coedcenlas
coetan	quoit	Carreg Goetan
coety	woodland, dwelling	Goety
corres	female dwarf	Llwyngorres
cors	bog, marsh	Castlemartin Corse
craig	rock, cliff	Craig-y-Creigwyr
crochan	cauldron	Pwllcrochan
croes	cross	Croesgoch
crogwydd	gallows	Cnwc-y-grogwydd
crug	tump, knoll	Crug-yr-hwch
crugiau	tumps, knolls	Crugiau Cemais
crwm	crooked, bent	Crymych
cwcwll	cowl	Quickwell
cwm	valley	Cwmyreglwys
cwmins	common	Cwmins Bach
cyfrwy	saddle	Carngyfrwy
dan	under, below	Danderi
dau	two	Daugleddau
deri	oak	Pwllderi
derwen	oak	Danydderwen
din(as)	hill fortress	Dinas
dôl	meadow	Dolrannog
dowrog	watery	Dowrog
drain	thorns	Llwyn-drain
drum see trum		
drysi	brambles	Tredrysi
du	black	Wern-ddu
dŵr	water	Dŵr Cleifion
dyffryn	valley	Parc-y-dyffryn
efail	smithy	Efail-fach
eglwys	church	Eglwyswrw
eithin	gorse	Cefneithin
esgair	long ridge	Esgair-ordd
fach see bach		
faenor see maenor		
fagwyr see magwyr		
fawr see mawr		

Welsh word	*English meaning*	*Example of place-name*
feidr *see* meidr		
felin *see* melin		
foel *see* moel		
freni *see* breni		
fron *see* bron		
ffald	fold	Y Ffald
ffordd	road, way	Pen-ffordd
ffos	ditch	Ffos-y-mynach
ffynnon	well	Ffynnon-gain
gafr	goat	Blaengafren
ganol *see* canol		
garn *see* carn		
gawsai *see* cawsai		
gelli *see* celli		
gilfach *see* cilfach		
glan	river bank	Glandwr
glas	green, blue	Ffynnon-las
glyn	valley	Glyn-maen
goch *see* coch		
godir	steep, slope	Godir-y-bwch
gors-	assembly place	Gors Fawr
groes *see* croes		
grug	heather	Tŷ-grug
gurnos	hilly place	Gurnos
gwaelod	bottom	Pwllgwaelod
gwastad	level	Gwastad
gwaun	moor	Cwmgwaun
gwennol	swallow	Plas-y-wennol
gwern	alder	Trewern
gwrach	witch	Pwll-y-wrach
gwrhyd	fathom, a width	Gwrhyd
gwylan	gull	Carreg-wylan
gwyn	white	Tŷ-gwyn
gwynt	wind	Penlan-wynt
haearn	iron	Pont-haearn
hafod	summer dwelling	Hafod Tydfil
haidd	barley	Haythog
hen	old	Henllys
hendre	winter dwelling	Hendre
hir	long	Tremaenhir
hydd	stag	Cnwc-yr-hydd
iet	gate	Tŷ'r Iet
isaf	lower	Treddafydd Isaf
las *see* glas		
lwyd *see* llwyd		
llain	narrow strip of land	Pen-llain
llan	church	Llan-non

Welsh word	English meaning	Example of place-name
llannerch	clearing, glade	Llannerch
llech	stone, rock	Llechydrybedd
llethr	slope	Llethr
llety	lodging, shelter	Llety'r Aderyn
llwch	lake	Lochtyrffin
llwyd	grey	Tŷ-llwyd
llwyn	tree	Llwyn-gwair
llygad	source	Llygadcleddau
llyn	lake	Blaen-llyn
llys	court	Llys-y-frân
maen	stone	Maen Sigl
maenor	manor	Maenorowen
maes	field, plain	Waun-maes
magwyr	wall	Fagwyr-las
marchog	knight	Tremarchog
mawr	great, big	Trellwyn-fawr
meidr	lane	Meidr Dywyll
meini	stones	Carn Meini
melin	mill	Felin Hescwm
melinau	mills	Meline
melindre	mill village	Velindre
melyn	yellow	Mynydd Melyn
moel	bare hill	Foel Cwmcerwyn
morfa	sea-marsh, fen	Morfa
mynach	monk	Ffos-y-mynach
mynachlog	monastery	Mynachlogddu
mynydd	mountain	Mynydd Du
nant	brook	Nant y Bugail
newydd	new	Tafarn Newydd
ogof	cave	Ogof Goetan
pall	covering, tent	Pallau
pant	hollow, valley	Pantyderi
parc	field, park	Parc y Meirw
pen	head, promontory	Penally
penglog	skull	Penybenglog
penrhyn	promontory	Penrhyn-ychen
pentre	village, homestead	Pentregalar
perllan	orchard	Y Berllan
pistyll	spout	Pistyll Meugan
plas	mansion, hall	Plas y Bridell
pont	bridge	Pont-iago
porth	harbour	Porthgain
portis	wattle fence, porch	Portis-bach
pren	wood	Pont-bren
pwll	pool, pit	Pwll-llong
pysgod	fish	Dinbych-y-pysgod
rhiw	hill	Pen-rhiw

Welsh word	*English meaning*	*Example of place-name*
rhos	moorland	Rhoscrowther
rhyd	ford	Glanrhyd
Saeson	Englishmen	Pont Saeson
Sais	Englishman	Iet Sais
strodur	pack-saddle	Pwllstrodur
sych	dry	Sychbant
tafarn	inn	Tafarn-bwlch
teg	fair	Pistyll-teg
tir	land	Tir-newydd
tirion	turf, country	Pant-tirion
traeth	beach, strand	Traeth Mawr
tref	town, homestead	Trefdraeth
tri	three	Tri-maen trai
trum	ridge	Y Drum
trwyn	point, cape	Trwyn Bwa
tŷ	house	Tŷddewi
tyddyn	smallholding	Tyddyn Castell
tywarch	turf, peat	Rhosdywarch
tywyn	sand dunes	Tywyn
uchaf	higher, upper	Pengegin uchaf
waun *see* gwaun		
wen *see* gwyn		
wern *see* gwern		
ŵyn	lambs	Clun-yr-ŵyn
y, yr, 'r	the	Yr Hendre
ydlan	hay guard	Ydlan Ddegwm
ynys	island	Ynys Cantwr
ysgubor	barn	Ysgubor-wen

BIBLIOGRAPHY

Barrett, John H.   *The Pembrokeshire Coast Path* HMSO (1974)
Davis, T. A. Warren   *Plants of Pembrokeshire* West Wales Naturalists' Trust
                            (Haverfordwest, 1970)
Evans, D. E.   *Pembrokeshire Coast Scenery* National Museum of Wales
                            (Cardiff, 1973)
Fraser, Maxwell   *Introducing West Wales* Methuen (1956)
Jennett, Sean   *South-West Wales* Darton, Longman & Todd (1967)
John, Brian   *Pembrokeshire* David & Charles (Newton Abbot, 1976)
Lockley, R. M.   *Pembrokeshire* Robert Hale (1957)
Miles, Dillwyn   *A Pembrokeshire Anthology* Hughes & Son (Llandybie, 1983)
    —   *Portrait of Pembrokeshire* Robert Hale (1984)
    —   *Pembrokeshire Coast National Park* HMSO (1972)
Moore, Donald   *The Land of Dyfed in Early Times* Cambrian Archaeological
                            Association (Cardiff, 1964)
Rees, Vyvyan   *Shell Guide to South-West Wales* Faber & Faber (1963)
Roberts, Tony   *A Guide to Walking the Pembrokeshire Coast Path*
                            Pembrokeshire Handbooks (Haverfordwest, 1976)
    —   *A Short Guide to the Best Walks in Pembrokeshire*
                            Pembrokeshire Handbooks (Fishguard, 1977)
Saunders, D.   *A Brief Guide to the Birds of Pembrokeshire* Five Arches
                            Press (Tenby, 1975)
Stark, Patrick   *Walking the Pembrokeshire Coast Path* Five Arches Press
                            (Tenby, 1974)
Stickings, Thos. G.   *Castles and Strongholds of Pembrokeshire* Five Arches Press
                            (Tenby, 1973)
Wight, M.   *Pembrokeshire and the National Park* H. G. Walters, Ltd
                            (1954)
Wright, Christopher   *A Guide to the Pembrokeshire Coast Path* Constable (1986)
Pembrokeshire Coast National Park publications include:
Ellis-Gruiffydd, S. D. *Coastal Scenery of the Pembrokeshire Coast National Park*
    —   *Rocks and Landforms of the Pembrokeshire Coast
                            National Park*
John, Brian   *Milford Haven Waterway*
    —   *Presely Hills*
Knights, Peter   *Birds of the Pembrokeshire Coast*
Kruys, Ivan   *Butterflies of Pembrokeshire*
Miles, Dillwyn   *Castles of Pembrokeshire*

INDEX
(Photographs in italics)